A MEMOIR

BY JERRY HELLER
WITH GIL REAVILL

SIMON SPOTLIGHT ENTERTAINMENT

New York | London | Toronto | Sydney

This is a work of nonfiction. I have done my best to tell this story the way it happened and, in many cases, clear up standing misconceptions and misunderstandings. Events and actions have been retold as I have remembered them. Conversations presented in dialogue form have been re-created based on my memory of them, but they are not intended to represent word-for-word documentation of what was said; rather, they are meant to evoke the substance of what was actually said.

Photographs on pages 12, 50, 80, 105, 145, 151, 159, 179, 206,
217, 246, 259, and 283 are from the author's collection.
Photograph on page 3 copyright © 2006 by Lynn Goldsmith
Photograph on page 26 courtesy of Alonzo Williams
Photograph on page 195 by Bleu Cotton Photography, www.bleucotton.com
Photograph on page 229 copyright © 2006 by Jim Britt, courtesy of Michael Ochs Archive
Photograph on page 274 copyright © 2006 by Michael Ochs Archive

SIMON SPOTLIGHT ENTERTAINMENT
An imprint of Simon & Schuster
1230 Avenue of the Americas, New York, New York 10020
Copyright © 2006 by Jerry Heller

SIMON SPOTLIGHT ENTERTAINMENT and related logo
are trademarks of Simon & Schuster, Inc.
Designed by Steve Kennedy
Manufactured in the United States of America
First Edition 10 9 8 7 6 5 4 3 2 1
Library of Congress Cataloging-in-Publication Data
Heller, Jerry, 1940–
Ruthless / by Jerry Heller with Gil Reavill.
p. cm.
Includes discography (p. 312)
ISBN-13: 978-1-4169-1792-2
ISBN-10: 1-4169-1792-6
1. Heller, Jerry, 1940– 2. Sound recording executives and producers—United States—Biography.
3. Ruthless Records (Firm). I. Reavill, Gil, 1953– II. Title.
ML429.H383A3 2006
781.64092—dc22
[B]
2006013857

For Gayle
And for Eazy

You are now about to witness the strength of street knowledge.

—first line, "Straight Outta Compton,"
N.W.A. (NIGGAZ WITH ATTITUDE)

ACKNOWLEDGMENTS

I want to dedicate this book to my wonderful wife, Gayle, the true love of my life, who stood beside me, with support and love and courage, during the Ruthless years. Gayle, you've made the past sixteen years a joy. This book is also for Dave and Hilda, and Joyce and Harry, who all died way too young. And it's for all the artists and fellow players who have helped form the recollections embodied in this work: My gratitude to all of you is heartfelt and sincere, and I want to thank you for inviting me to be a part of your careers and lives. Most especially, *Ruthless* is for Eric Wright, the quintessential little big man.

This book could not have been created without the participation of three extremely talented people: Gil Reavill, who captured the essence of my story; and at Simon & Schuster's Simon Spotlight Entertainment imprint, publisher Jen Bergstrom and editor Tricia Boczkowski, both brilliant at guiding me through an unfamiliar process. I'd also like to thank all those who helped jog my memory and keep it real: Gary Ballen, Phyllis Pollack, Julio G, Doug Young, Andrew Klein, Bret Saxon, Don Fischel, Lester Knispel, Kim Kenner Wash, Phil Casey, Jack Kellman, Ron Delsener, Atron Gregory, Alonzo Williams, Irving Azoff. Special thanks to Michael Nadeau for making the connection.

CAST OF CHARACTERS

Eazy-E

aka Eric Wright, my friend, surrogate son, and partner, founder and sole proprietor of Ruthless Records, founder and member of N.W.A., prime mover and "conceptualizer" of gangsta rap, died of AIDS March 26, 1995, bringing an end to the Ruthless era

Dr. Dre

aka Andre Young, premier genius of rap, member of N.W.A., producer of Snoop Dogg, Eminem, 50 Cent, the Game, cofounder of Death Row Records

Ice Cube

aka O'Shea Jackson, poet laureate of rap, member of N.W.A., movie star and Hollywood power player

BACKUP PLAYERS

DJ Yella

aka Antoine Carraby, member of N.W.A., producing partner of Dr. Dre in High Powered Productions, successful producer of adult films

MC Ren

aka Lorenzo Patterson, member of N.W.A., running partner to Eazy-E, great rapper

Arabian Prince

aka Mik Lezan, Kim Nazel, original member of N.W.A., smooth-as-silk producer

NEMESIS

Suge Knight

aka Marion Knight Jr., bodyguard, felon, cofounder of Death Row Records

SUPPORTING ACTS

The D.O.C

aka Tracy "Trey" Curry, hip-hop's best natural rapper, lyricist, "Fifth Beatle" in N.W.A.

Michel'le

aka Michelle Toussaint, Ruthless R&B songstress

Bone Thugs-N-Harmony

Top-selling post-N.W.A. Ruthless act

Above the Law

Ruthless-signed rap group, heir apparent to N.W.A.

CAMEOS

Alonzo Williams

World Class Wreckin' Cru founder, promoter, producer

Julio G . . . Greg Mack . . . Tony G . . .

Early rap radio pioneers and original KDAY mixmasters

N.W.A. in the Efil4zaggin period: Ren, Eazy, Dre, Yella

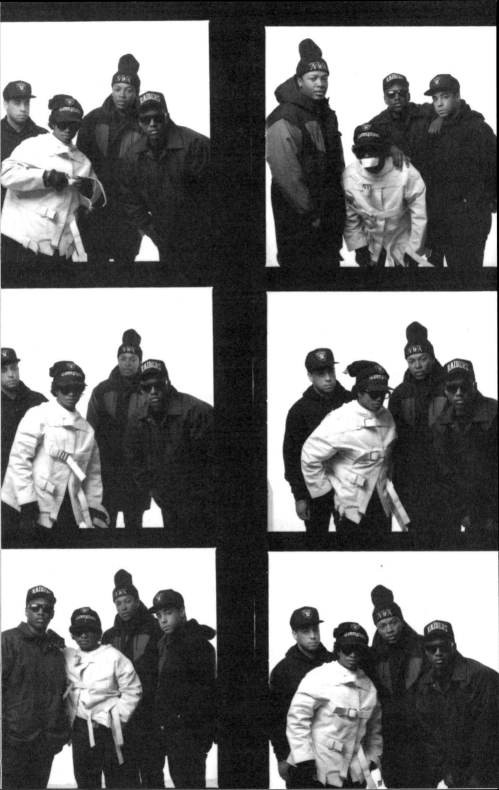

So if a nigga ever try to Jerry Hellin' me
Tell Dre put up a mil' cause that's what my bail will be
— THE GAME, "NO MORE FUN AND GAMES"

Dissed by the best. Jerry Heller, urban legend and all-purpose straw dog of the hip-hop world. I'm the boogey man used to scare South Central kids when they tell ghost stories.

In the late 1990s, I recall meeting a young Dallas rapper named JR Ewng, just like the *Dallas* character, only without the *i*. This was in downtown L.A. at the offices of Hit A Lick Records, a Latino rap label I was helping to start.

"Hey, how you doing, man?" I said as I was introduced. JR had a stricken look on his face. It turned out he thought he was meeting the devil.

"I had heard on the streets that Jerry Heller was the Antichrist, Lucifer, the whole nine," JR recalled. "The story in the rap community was that Heller was the White Devil, enemy to the black man. He would steal, lie, and kill, whatever it took to ruin the black man. And as I walked into his office, I started to believe the hype."

But I was nothing like JR was expecting. I treated him with respect and listened to what he had to say. We had a good meeting.

As he was leaving, JR turned back for one last comment: "People had me thinking that I was coming to meet the devil. You don't look like no devil to me." The whole office busted out with laughter. JR and I have a warm, respectful relationship to this day.

When the writer Hunter S. Thompson was transformed into Uncle Duke in *Doonesbury*, he always used to complain on lecture tours that no guidebooks existed to instruct you on how to live your life once you have been made into a comic-strip character. It was as though *Doonesbury* creator Gary Trudeau had somehow stolen a piece of Hunter Thompson's soul, like a rain forest native who refuses to be photographed.

Likewise, there are no guides or advice available on what to do now that I have been made into the Great Satan. What's my move? How can I possibly respond?

For a long time, I did what any self-respecting Great Satan would do. I kept quiet. I didn't care what Dre or Cube or the D.O.C. said about me—even when they lied publicly that I had stolen money from them, ripped them off, cheated them. To me, their snaps were easy to dismiss. If I had stolen from them, why hadn't they ever sued me? I knew who I was, and I knew what had really gone down.

Then a guy named Big Reg, Reggie Turner, now in prison for various financial misdealings, told me a home truth that stayed in my mind.

"You know, the way it works on the street," Big Reg said, "if you don't answer a rumor, people believe it's fact."

A rumor undenied is deemed true. Over time, the idea dogged at me. I never deigned to deny any of the rumors Cube and Suge and the others were spreading about me, so those rumors had assumed the status of gospel truth in the hood.

"You can't be the Nigga 4 Life crew with a white Jew telling you what to do," raps Ice Cube on his track "No Vaseline."

Ugly, but there it is.

How do I answer? By going into the hood, getting up on a soapbox? Pointing out that yes, I am indeed a white Jew, but no, I didn't tell Eazy-E what to do—he was always my boss, I was never his?

What am I supposed to do, answer rap with rap? Eazy once said that he thought I was the second most famous person in rap, and he wanted to do a record with me because it would sell a lot of copies. Ladies and gentlemen, I give you MC "White Jew" Heller:

Gangsta pranksta
Always hatin' and baitin'
Paintin' me like I'm the Great Satan
Just 'cause I'm a Jew
And you don't know what else to do
So you go emetic
And anti-Semitic
And the choke on your jokes
Is set on automatic
A Hip-Hopalong Cassidy
Whose weapon is mendacity
But you're toothless
Because the truth is Ruthless
It ain't hard it's Eazy
And the truth is what frees me
I ain't a hater
I'm an educator
And an illustrator
As dope as Tommy Chong
Teaching you Wright from wrong

Yes, well . . . it's pretty clear I won't be topping the charts as a rapper anytime soon.

But I know the truth, and the truth is in this book. It's my truth, but it's also Eazy's truth, the best that I can tell it. From the first day we met, until his last months, when he was too weak from illness to resist the vultures among those who crowded around his deathbed, we had a relationship built on all the finest qualities of human interaction: trust, empathy, respect, humor, and love.

Eazy-E saw his best friend, the brilliant Andre Young, Dr. Dre, betray him. They had come up together on the violent streets of Compton. O'Shea Jackson, aka Ice Cube, another artist of transcendent talent, also turned on Eazy with casual viciousness, ridiculing him, dissing him repeatedly, battering him in rap after rap.

Betrayal, well, that's as human as breathing. "A good friend," says Oscar Wilde, "is one who stabs you in the front." But I never betrayed Eric Wright, and while he was in full possession of his faculties, he never betrayed me. If that's a kind of brotherhood that threatens some people, so be it.

Eric, this one's for you, my brother.

Eazy-E and me

GANGSTA GANGSTA

Intelligence is the relative inability to be surprised

I

This is the way Eazy-E always told it:

A voice of an old friend filters through Eazy's cell phone—smooth, reassuring.

"Hey, yo, you know we got to work this shit out," Dr. Dre says.

Eazy doesn't give him anything, just grunts. He has three cell phones and several beepers; he's always juggling them. That night one of his multiple girlfriends is calling him over and over on his little Motorola mobile.

"This is important," Dr. Dre says. "You want to get with me up here?"

Long pause while Eazy thinks. There's something strange in Dre's voice. "Where you at?" he finally says.

"S.O.L.A.R.," says Dre. The Galaxy Studios of S.O.L.A.R., Sounds of Los Angeles Records, ex–Soul Train producer and record exec Dick Griffey's place on the grimy edge of Hollywood, near where the 101 freeway heads up over Cahuenga Pass toward Universal.

April 23, 1991, a Tuesday night. Eazy's rolling alone in his white BMW 850ci all the way over on the West Side. A sprinkle of spring rain splashed across Los Angeles, just enough to darken the pavement.

"'Kay," Eazy says. "I'm right around the corner."

"I'll be here," Dr. Dre says.

Eazy flips one phone shut, at the same time opening the Motorola to deal with his girlfriend.

Like a lot of betrayals, this one comes disguised as a peace offering. Eazy-E's Ruthless Records holds Dre's contract as a producer, rapper, and writer. Dre is restless. A lot of people are whispering in his ear. Get out of Ruthless, they're saying. You're getting ripped off. There's a whole host of Dre whisperers, but one main one: Suge Knight, a former bodyguard of Dre's who is itching to set himself up as a record executive.

So tonight Dre calls Eazy offering to "work this shit out." Just two homies working through their differences. They know each other from way back, from coming up in Compton. Eazy already is offering Dre the fucking moon. Produce anybody you want, work with anyone you want. Just don't kill the golden goose, don't drop out of N.W.A. What would be the sense of that? The group is pulling down tens of millions of dollars a year.

It takes Eazy more than three hours before he finally arrives at Galaxy. He's famous for that. He is constantly telling people, I'll be right there, I'm right near to you, and then he shows up six hours later. What happens during those hours? What could the guy possibly do? No one knows for sure. It's a mystery. But whatever he's doing, and Dre knows this well, it probably has something to do with pussy.

Eazy always likes to roll alone. Anywhere, everywhere,

South Central, his home streets of Compton, Norwalk, Inglewood, the Valley, the barrio, the West Side beaches. Roscoe's, Fatburger, Friday's. Usually no bodyguards. When he does have security, they meet him places, they rarely drive with him. The little dude (he stands all of five feet two) is fearless.

The traffic flows up over the pass, a parade of red taillights disappearing one after another. Eazy parks his ride on Cahuenga. But when he enters the building and heads up to the third floor of the wood-and-glass Galaxy studios, the place feels wrong, deserted.

No Dre.

Instantly Eazy realizes that he has been set up.

Suge Knight walks into the studio through the control room door, and he brings along muscle. A pair of them, big-shouldered guys, each carrying a Louisville Slugger, handling the maple bats as if they are toothpicks. Eazy never does learn the names of the batboys.

He would be able to do the math in his head and figure out that between Suge and his two wheel-chock muscleboys, he was outweighed maybe ten pounds of theirs to every one of his.

Eazy plays it cold. This is just street shit, and he's been there before, plenty of times. This is a robbery, a jacking. He slides into a black leather captain's chair. Listens to Suge tell him what he has to do to walk out of that room alive.

"You got to sign these," Suge says. He holds up three sheets of paper, three releases—one each for Dre, the D.O.C., and the best-selling R&B singer Michel'le, Dre's girlfriend, each one with the fax imprint of Sony legal. Sony owns S.O.L.A.R., and desperately wants the hotter-than-a-pistol Dre on its roster. The label is willing to make a deal with the devil—aka Suge Knight—to sign Dre.

Problem is, Dre ain't free. He's signed to Eazy and Ruthless. He's not even a solo act yet, just a beat maker, but his genius and worth are beginning to be recognized.

"What you rollin' with tonight, that Chevy dualie of yours? Or the seven-fifty?" Suge asks.

Eazy, stone-faced.

"You see a white van parked down there on the street?" That's a detail Eazy notices: Suge says "white van," as though it's somehow important that it's white.

"We got Jerry Heller tied up in the back of that van, gun to his head, blow his goddamn fucking brains out."

Eazy doubts it, but it's not like Suge isn't capable of doing something like that. Then Suge adds a kicker. "We can get your moms, too. You want us to?"

Eazy has a quick flash of the two people he is closest to in the world, bound together in the back of some ratty Ford Econoline. Again, he doesn't really believe it, but the image unsettles him.

Suge has a slight, almost buttery voice, not harsh at all. The bluster is provided by the steady slap of maple behind him.

"You better off signing," Suge says.

Eazy signs.

II

Like I said, that's the story Eazy always told, including in connection with our suit against Suge, Dre, and Sony Records. Dre has never denied making the phone call, but always insisted he had nothing to do with what transpired that night at Galaxy. Our suit was settled out of court.

Where was I during all this? Where was Eazy's mentor and confidante, his stalwart defender, the guy Eazy hired to make sure the burgeoning empire of Ruthless Records ran smoothly? How did I spend that evening of April 23, 1991?

Well, I wasn't tied up in the back of a van with Eric Wright's fifty-year-old Montessori-school-teaching mother.

While Suge Knight was dealing with Eazy-E that evening, I had already settled in at home in Calabasas, reading a Stuart Woods thriller. I had no idea what was going down just across the Santa Monica foothills from me.

In a very real sense, though, I was at Eric's side that night, hearing the slap of the bats along with him. Intelligence, I've read, is the relative inability to be surprised. Since I always prided myself in being one of the smartest guys I had ever met, I constantly tried to anticipate anything that might happen in any given situation, in order to cut down on my chances of ever being surprised.

So I had already imagined that Suge might make a move such as this, and had spoken with Eric over and over about what he was going to do when it happened.

The first time we talked about it was six months earlier, at three a.m. in the kitchen of my house in the Valley.

Eric and I kept very different hours. He always had the key to my place, and many times I would wake to hear him moving

"Oh, man, that's cold, him making you do that."

"No, see, why I told you that story: That's how real friends in music do business with each other. You work things out."

"You took a big hit," Eazy said. "Bruce Springsteen."

"I told Freddie, 'This one's on me,'" I said to Eazy. "Look, all I'm telling you is that if Suge and Dre come at us friendly, try-ing to work with us, maybe we can do something with them."

"Only they ain't going to come at us friendly," Eric said. And he was right.

In trying to get into the music business, Suge made a crucial mistake, one that would come to haunt him. He had entered a new, unfamiliar world, a world controlled by the rule of law, and he didn't realize it. He thought he was still on the street, and that street tactics (the only ones he knew) would somehow translate to the world of business.

"Listen, Eric," I repeated to Eazy, "you've got to promise me—don't get fucking killed over this, don't even take a beat down. Just sign the goddamn release and we'll work the whole thing out later with the lawyers."

No reply. Stone-faced.

Then: "I think we should kill him."

I couldn't believe it. I sat there, momentarily at a loss. Looking at him, I could tell he was dead serious. I had not a shred of doubt that he had the means, the connections, the will to follow up. If Eazy-E wanted Marion Knight dead and he wasn't talked out of it, then Marion Knight would be killed.

"Um, let's just think this through," I finally said. "We're doing millions a month in business with only six employees. I mean, we're doing really well, we have a lot of money coming in."

Eric didn't seem to make the connection between what I was

saying and what he had just suggested. "All the more reason," he said.

"No, man, no," I said. "Maybe I'm just not a wartime consigliere, but none of this makes any sense to me. You're a *success*," I said, emphasizing the word as though he might not fully realize what it meant. "You made it, man. You want to throw it all away by killing some guy?"

So I talked with him, bringing up various scenarios repeatedly over the next few months. We spoke about it four or five times over that winter and spring. If Suge did this, what would be our move? With my conspiratorial mind-set, I could imagine the Suge Knight camp conducting a campaign of drive-bys, ambushes, phone threats, intimidation of Ruthless artists, random acts of commercial terrorism. I laid it all out to Eazy. And always, I told him over and over that it wasn't worth jeopardizing his life just to show who could outfront whom.

The message must have gotten through, because Eazy's natural impulse that damp night in April would have been to come out of the bag at Suge Knight. It didn't matter, outweighed ten to one or a hundred to one—that was just the way Eric Wright had always been. It was an attitude pounded into him by Compton: Fight, no matter what, to the bitter end. He was like that mouse in the cartoon, about to die with the eagle's talons screaming down on him, defiantly giving the middle finger as his last act on Earth.

But that night at the Galaxy studios, he took my advice, signed Dre's release and the releases of the D.O.C. and Michel'le, and lived to fight another day. And I still think he was right to do it that way.

In another sense, though, I failed him. Eric Wright had hired me as sort of a superbodyguard—not for his physical self (he had other people for that) but for his business. One of my duties, whether clearly articulated or not, was to protect the life of the goose that laid the golden egg: N.W.A., a rap supergroup, the black Beatles. I acted as the general manager of Ruthless Records, so that had to be my ultimate goal, a mandate so obvious that it didn't even need to be spelled out.

And I failed. I failed because I couldn't imagine anyone coming in between the two most crucial members of the group— Eazy-E and Dr. Dre. I couldn't grasp the idea that two people could be that tight, could have that much history, could reach the pinnacle of fame and success together, and then have one turn around and betray the other. I didn't have that level of understanding of the human animal. I guess that even after the three decades I had spent in the rough-and-tumble music business, in a corner of my soul I was still naive.

One problem was that I was having too much fun to think someone might bust up the party.

We all were. It was the early 1990s, and N.W.A. was the hippest, most popular act in America, lionized as "the world's most dangerous band." The checks rained down on Ruthless Records like slot machine payoffs. The five members—Eazy-E, Dr. Dre, Ice Cube, DJ Yella, MC Ren—were all young guys, none over twenty-five, some barely out of high school, who were making money for the first time in their lives.

I once walked into Dre's house when he was living near me in a gated community in Calabasas. He had asked me to go through a few things with him, check his business mail, straighten out some accounting.

I opened a desk drawer, stuffed full of papers. I started going through it, and found an uncashed check for twelve thousand dollars.

"Hey, Andre? What the fuck is this?" Digging deeper into the drawer, I discovered that there were several others. I couldn't believe it. I tore open envelopes from ASCAP and BMI, from various acts or producers, dated weeks or months previous. Tens of thousands of dollars total, monies for his much-in-demand services as a beat maker, writer, and producer. Meanwhile, the guy was constantly pleading poverty.

Dre looked at me with a soft smile and shrugged. "I guess stuff kinda gets away from me," he said.

Nothing compares to that first rush of crazed, unhinged excitement of having real money when you are young. The members of N.W.A. were buying BMWs, buying diamond studs the size of marbles, buying MCM and Fila and Gucci. Dre, Eazy, and I used to jockey over which of us would get to take Michel'le shopping, just for the pure splurging joy of it. It was as though she had a boyfriend, brother, and father all competing to spend money on her.

They gained entry into places that had previously been denied to them. The act of buying a car had been transformed from a humiliating, esteem-shredding experience into one during which they were fawned over and toadied up to. Instead of getting hassled at the door of nightclubs for wearing running shoes, they were treated like superstars and ushered into the VIP sections.

I took them to top L.A. restaurants, such as the Palm, Trumps, Monty's, Ivy at the Shore. Few experiences are as pleasurable as watching someone tear apart a lobster for the first time in their lives.

Even back then, I realized that all that action was bound to attract predators. I thought I would be ready for them. It was like we were all partying around the bonfire, and somewhere out there in the darkness a bear was prowling, hungry but too afraid of the flames to actually come in and attack: Marion Knight. "Sugar Bear." So nicknamed by his father, a truck driver, because, he said, his son was so sweet.

When Suge Knight made the move into rap, rap stopped being fun. In the spring of 1991, Eazy and I weren't seeing much of the "sugar" in Marion Knight. He was all about showing us the bear. To us, he was Marion the Barbarian. We found ourselves at war. I had just turned fifty, and my life suddenly turned into a personal Vietnam.

When I left the Ruthless offices on Burbank Boulevard in the San Fernando Valley suburb of Woodland Hills, I never drove home the same route twice. I employed two mountainous bodyguards, Animal and MD. These guys both looked like NFL offensive guards, which MD actually was at one time. When I rolled up to my house in the northern L.A. suburbs, one of my bodyguards would usually go in first, to make sure the place was secure. Only then would I be able to enter my own home.

But even at that point, I couldn't relax. I kept loaded guns all over the house: a .25 Colt double action automatic in a secret drawer in a Chinese prayer table near my front door; an ivory-handled .32-caliber within reach of my backyard Jacuzzi; a .12-gauge Remington standing upright in my bedroom closet.

I slept with a big .380 Beretta underneath my pillow. At times at night I would be jolted awake by the inadvertent touch of the cold carbon steel, like an emergency wake-up call, indicating that there just might be trouble in paradise.

Eighteen hours after Suge Knight had obtained releases

from Eazy that effectively meant the end of N.W.A., he faxed Sony Records from S.O.L.A.R. Dr. Dre, the most sought-after producer in rap, Suge's message stated, was now under his exclusive control.

"Dear Hank" was the mock-formal language Suge used to communicate the change to Hank Caldwell of Sony. "Andre Young is available to do your projects now."

It was "imperative," Suge wrote to Caldwell, that Sony immediately forward $102,750 to his company, Knight Life Productions—an entity that would eventually mutate into Death Row Records.

It's a bad thought of mine, I know, an unworthy one, and one that I am thoroughly ashamed about. But I can't help that there's a small, niggling voice in the back of my mind, telling me that I could have saved everyone a whole lot of grief.

"I think we should kill him," Eazy had said.

Maybe I should have just turned my back that night and let Eazy-E do what he wanted to do.

The days of lace and satin: Alonzo, Yella, Dre, and Shakespeare of the World Class Wreckin' Cru, with Mona Lisa Young

STRAIGHT OUTTA COMPTON

You have to step ahead to prevent yourself
from falling behind

I

A half decade earlier, in the mid-1980s, before I had ever met Eric Wright, my life hit a bad patch. My first marriage had just flamed out in divorce. I was reeling, personally and professionally.

So I tucked my tail between my legs and moved in with my parents in Encino. I slept on a foldaway bed in their condo. I moved there not because I was down and out—I wasn't—but because I wanted to be around people who cared about me; I didn't feel like being on my own.

Still, when I woke up groggy and stared around at the world from my mother's floral print sofa, it wasn't exactly an esteem booster. I couldn't help but feel a shade depressed. *I'm almost forty-five years old,* I told myself, *and I'm back living with my parents again.*

I never worried about money. I knew I could always pull down a comfortable living. But as I sat in my Jockeys on my mom's couch, hungover from generous transfusions the night before of

Show us the money: Ruthless artists Po' Broke and Lonely with Dre

Angeles. Once he booked the Queen Mary, in permanent dock in Long Beach Harbor, for a dance. When I met him, he worked a new Compton club called Eve After Dark, bringing his crew of DJs down to spin Friday nights, booking some acts, creating a sort of rolling weekly party scene.

As soon as we met, Lonzo started bugging me to come down to his club and meet his "guys." His "guys" were a half dozen beat makers and mixmasters that he had first called Disco Construction, and then, after "disco" became something of a dirty word, changed their name to World Class Wreckin' Cru. Lonzo was one of the smart ones: He put his group's product out on his own label, Kru-Cut Records, using Macola only for pressing and distribution.

Alonzo asked me to manage the Wreckin' Cru and some other acts on Kru-Cut, including a group called C.I.A., for Crew In Action. By the beginning of 1986, a few months after I first walked through the doors at Macola, I was representing a majority of the artists on the scene. I had already pulled down $250,000. I guess I wasn't going to be doomed to have a $250,000 economic ceiling after all.

There were a few Macola artists who had other representation. A guy named Jay King represented a very popular group called the Timex Social Club. King wrote and produced the Social Club's "Rumors," one of the biggest twelve-inch releases ever. Macola was also pressing a seminal L.A. rapper at that time, Ice-T. I was drawn to Ice's stuff because it had a dangerous political edge that I thought was exciting. But Ice was already well on his way, driving a Rolls, very much on top of his business, with two very capable guys watching out for him, his manager, Jorge Hinojosa, and his tour guy, Charlie Jam.

Although I didn't sense it right away, Alonzo's main difficulty was that he was a little behind the times. Or rather, he was *of* the times. In the music business, it's like *Alice in Wonderland*: You have to be a step ahead to prevent yourself from falling behind. Just keeping pace with the crowd is a prescription for getting trampled.

So what would a just-keeping-pace kind of guy like Alonzo Williams be into back then? This was the mid-1980s. What were the two most influential acts around at that time?

If you are Alonzo Williams, the five-hundred-pound gorillas of the day are Prince and Michael Jackson. Megamillion sellers—in the case of Jackson's 1982 *Thriller*, an astounding forty-five million in sales worldwide. Prince's movie *Purple Rain* debuted in theaters in 1984. They were both huge in slightly different ways. Michael, the self-proclaimed "King of Pop," was the people's choice, while Prince was more the critic's darling.

Keeping careful pace with the tastes of the day, Lonzo dressed the Wreckin' Cru in the style of Prince Rogers Nelson, in matching outfits of lavender satin, with sequined touches and lace gloves. Since Lonzo had started off as a dancer, he paid particular attention to choreography, modeling his groups after the Temptations. He synchronized the Wreckin' Cru's moves onstage behind the turntables, using elaborate stylized moves that were straight out of Morris Day and the Time and the "Beat It" music video. That was *it* in those days.

Another guy hanging around Macola and mining a similar vein was an Oakland dancer named MC Hammer, who would hit superstar status in 1990 with "U Can't Touch This." I always liked Hammer. I never managed him, because he had his own team from Oakland handling that, but we were very friendly. He was one of the true gentlemen of the business, certainly one of the most open and genial artists I met at Macola in those days. I could always talk to him, just like I could always talk to Alonzo Williams.

But Hammer and Alonzo were both a little too poppy for me. I came up in the music business during the sixties, when popular music was split into two realms, like in the Bible, the separation of the sheep and the goats. AM radio sheep and FM radio goats. AM radio meant groups such as the Grass Roots and Gary Puckett and the Union Gap. With FM you entered waters that were a little deeper, a little murkier: Janis Joplin and Big Brother, the Grateful Dead, and bands such as that. It was also a question of Los Angeles versus San Francisco, the effete arty S.F. types looking down through their granny glasses at the "money-grubbers" from L.A.

Back then I usually worked both sides of the fence, but my heart was with Jimi and Janis. I have always felt closer to underground, closer to the edge, closer to new movements in music. Hammer struck me as mainstream. Alonzo Williams was also more mainstream.

I liked them both and I liked what they did. Lonzo had an appreciation of local tradition that few live-in-the-moment gangbangers could match. He bought the former house of Central Avenue hepcat Johnny Otis. I respected that.

The Wreckin' Cru, synchronized behind the turntables, dancing in color-coordinated lace. MC Hammer, another dance-oriented act, performing loopy, attenuated pirouettes in gold lamé parachute pants that looked as though they came straight out of a Turkish harem. Funk-based pop, theatrically staged. The audience, weaned on Prince and Michael Jackson, loved it.

But not all of the performers did. Lonzo had a young DJ in the Wreckin' Cru who was restless. So restless, in fact, that he would eventually trash the lavender suit, jump ship, and change the whole face of modern popular music.

IV

"Lonzo brought in Run-D.M.C.," Dr. Dre told me. "I think it was their first time in L.A., you know? And that was it. That was just it for me."

In 1984, a very young Andre Young started hanging out at Eve After Dark, bugging Alonzo Williams to let him do some cutting on the Cru. He was fresh out of high school in Compton. Lonzo finally let him in for a simple reason.

"He's absolute magic with women, man," Lonzo told me, raising an eyebrow. "Ladies fucking love him."

Once in the Wreckin' Cru, Young formed an alliance with a stocky DJ named Antoine Carraby, who used the stage monicker of DJ Yella. Andre Young needed a handle too so he modified the nickname of one of his heroes, Julius Erving, the legendary Dr. J of the Philadelphia 76ers, a basketball great who was among the top players in the game at the time. Dr. J pioneered the modern, above-the-rim playing style.

Dre always told me he liked Dr. J because he was forever number one in the NBA in steals. "I thought that was cool."

So Andre Young became Dr. Dre, the official resident lady-killer of Alonzo Williams's World Class Wreckin' Cru. On the Cru, he and Yella hung together, and when Lonzo brought Run-D.M.C. into Eve After Dark, the lightning bolt struck them both at the same time.

Conclusion number one, Dre and Yella standing there on their own turf, in their home club, listening to the crew from Hollis, Queens: "Damn, this shit is fresh."

Conclusion number two: "We could do this shit."

Conclusion number three: "Fuck the Cru. Fuck this shit.

Fuck Alonzo and his motherfucking synchronized dance moves and his corny outfits."

Entirely unintentionally, Lonzo had killed the Cru. He was the one who brought Joey Simmons, Darryl McDaniels, and Jason Mizell (aka Run, D.M.C., and Jam Master Jay) in front of his two young protégés. In the summer of 1984, Run-D.M.C.'s "It's Like That" had blown away everything else that came before in rap—the first hard-core rap song.

Genius leaps. Dr. Dre didn't have to think about it. Watching Run-D.M.C. at Eve After Dark, he had immediately grasped what he wanted to do.

I wasn't there the night Hollis, Queens, showed the way. Not my scene. But that didn't mean I wasn't just as restless as Andre Young. The Cru was okay. And all the rest of the acts I was managing were *okay*. But it was as if I was listening to the Beatles and waiting on the Rolling Stones. What I was doing back then was looking for something a little . . . harder. And it turned out so was Andre Young.

Looking for something harder. That's how I spent my time through the winter of 1986–87. Booking Lonzo and Dr. Dre and DJ Yella and the rest of the Cru in venues like Skateland—a Los Angeles roller-skating emporium that doubled as a concert venue in those days—and trying to get my acts on the radio.

Steve Yano's booth at the Roadium represented our major local distribution outlet. The real scene in L.A. was the roving bands of DJs that played parties all over south county and the Valley. The Wreckin' Cru and the Dream Team were prominent, but there were the Mixmasters and Uncle Jam's Army, too.

Three of the DJs from the Mixmasters got hired at KDAY, a

low-powered radio station with studios located at the top of Alvarado Street, in Echo Park. Julio G, Gregg Mack, and Tony G started playing rap, hosting interview shows, contributing mightily to the visibility of the West Coast rap scene in general and the artists I was representing out of Macola in particular.

KDAY became one of the true major players in the record business, but the station did so without wasting money on excess wattage. It was a lo-fi, low-rent, low-rise kind of enterprise. I'd be tuned into KDAY in the car on my way home to the Valley, 1580 on the AM band, and as I would drive over the Cahuenga Pass the signal would begin to drift a mere ten miles from the transmitter. One second I'd be listening to the World Class Wreckin' Cru doing "Juice," and all of sudden I'd hear Kenny Rogers break in from a more powerful country station in the Valley.

You got to know when to hold 'em, know when to fold 'em . . .

But Mack and the Two Gs became some of the most important players contributing to the rise of West Coast rap. I came to see KDAY as an almost mystical entity. Julio would play a Dream Team cut on that dim bulb of a radio station, and the next day Don MacMillan would get orders for ten, twenty, thirty thousand records—orders not just from KDAY's listening radius (which was, after all, about a four-block area of Echo Park), but from all over the country: Texas, Philadelphia, New York.

I could never figure out how it happened. But in the mid-1980s, KDAY was the electronic embodiment of the mysterious power called "word on the street."

Concerts in roller-skating rinks. A distribution model in which car trunks figured prominently. A single-station radio network with a signal that wavered in a high wind. When MacMillan got the orders and the money came in, Lonzo and the Cru and Rudy and whoever else had a piece of the pie would all head down to the corner of Santa Monica and Vine to divvy up the proceeds. I was the only one with a checking account, so I'd cash the check and meet them. We'd split up the money right there on the corner, usually twenty or thirty thousand dollars. A few times we had a one-hundred-thousand-dollar check to split.

Up Vine Street at Capitol, or over the hump at Warner Brothers in Burbank, they were doing business their own way. Down in the flats at Macola, we did it our way. I was loving it, happier than I have ever been, I think, in the record business. Joe Smith or David Geffen might have looked at me as though I were nuts, but I couldn't help it. I was down in the trenches with the little guys. This was just my kind of thing.

There were always people tugging at my sleeve. "Hey, Jerry," Lonzo said to me in early 1987. "I got this Compton guy keeps saying he wants to meet you."

"Yeah? A rapper?"

"Nah," Lonzo said. "He's like a street guy, got a lot of big ideas. He says he wants to start a record store or something."

"Hey, Lonzo, spare me, okay? I get a lot of people wanting to go into business with me. If I talked to all of them, I'd be in the business of going into business with people, you know what I mean? I wouldn't have time for anything else."

But the dude wouldn't quit. Every couple of weeks Lonzo would be back at it, saying this Compton guy wants to know me. A couple times I blew up at him.

"You owe this guy money or something? He your relative? Leave it alone!"

Part of my playing hard to get was a conscious business strategy. As an executive you erect a wall around yourself. You want to give yourself a little peace and quiet and cut down on distraction. But the wall serves another function, too. It weeds out the losers. It's Darwinian. If a supplicant is strong enough and resourceful enough to get through to me, maybe, just maybe, he's got something worthwhile to show me.

In spring of 1987 Lonzo was still hocking me. "Hey, man, you got to see this Compton guy. He's on me all the time about it."

"So? That's your problem." I walked away from him.

He followed. "Listen, Jerry, the guy says he'll pay me for an introduction to you."

I stopped and turned back around. "How much?"

"Seven hundred and fifty." Lonzo paused. "Truth, Jerry, I could use the money."

That didn't necessarily sway me. Lonzo was a friend, but I don't think there was ever a time when he couldn't use $750. For him, saying he needed money was like saying "I'm breathing." On the other hand, it did intrigue me that someone was willing to pay cash money for an introduction to me.

"Who is this guy again?"

He had told me before, but I wasn't really listening, so he told me again.

"All right," I said. "I'll be back around next week."

"When?" Lonzo wanted to know.

"Tuesday afternoon, three thirty."

I could tell he wanted me to bump up the date a little, advance his payday. But he didn't push it.

listened to Eric Wright laying out "the plan." People were for-ever laying out "the plan" to me. Usually it involved conquering the entertainment industry, though I got the idea some people would just as soon go ahead and aim for world domination. Everybody, every single person, was going to hit the charts like Elvis, bring 'em to their knees like Sinatra, reinvent the wheel like Hendrix.

But I reacted differently to Eric's pitch. He wasn't rushed, or gushing. He never took his hat or sunglasses off. He just very calmly told me what he was going to do.

"I want to start my own label," he said. A place where an artist could work without anyone looking over his shoulder, telling him what he could and could not do—a free environ-ment, no rules, no catering to any taste other than the artist's own.

I held off saying what I usually said at this point, which was that he was the sixth, twelfth, twentieth person this week, month, year that had stepped up and told me they wanted to start a business with me.

Instead I asked him again, "You want to play me something?"

Eazy fished out a tape from the front pocket of his jacket. He slotted it into the conference room's deck and played me a song called "Boyz-N-the-Hood."

Cruisin' down the street in my 6-4
Jockin' the bitches, slappin' the ho's . . .

The whole story rolled out in a distinctive nasal whine, a South Central saga, a day in the thug life. Driving in Compton, witnessing jackings, blasting back at enemies, pulling up at police actions and jail riots. A blistering view of a harsh world. Always coming back again and again to the chorus.

'Cause the boys in the hood are always hard
You come talkin' that trash, we'll pull ya card

I thought it was the most important rap music I had ever heard. This was the Rolling Stones, the Black Panthers, Gil Scott-Heron; this was music that would change everything.

Wow.

"Wow" is the word.

If I play it today, I can still hear the "wow" in "Boyz-N-the-Hood." No apologies, no excuses, just the straight undistilled street telling me things I had never heard before, yet that I understood instantly.

The voice that delivered the rap was maddening. When I first heard it, I immediately wanted to dismiss it, tell Eric, *Shit, this guy isn't a rapper. First thing we do is hire a professional. I know a real good MC. . . .*

But then it hit me. It was him. Eazy-E himself was doing the rapping.

"Who is that?" I asked. He didn't answer. "Was that you?"

I asked him to play it again, and he did.

The rap wasn't professional, it wasn't smooth, but it grew on me. Eazy's voice was as insistent as the ghetto—you wanted to deny its reality, but you just couldn't. The timbre and style of his rapping was wholly original. It kept insinuating itself into my brain like a nail file. "Racky" we would have called it back when I was growing up in Cleveland, from "racketeer." I've heard his voice called a lot of things since that first day I heard it, but it was always "racky" to me. It sounded as though the rapper came straight out of the state home for wayward youths.

There are three qualities I've tabulated that can lift an act to superstardom. The first is actually to be the first, a trailblazer or innovator, like Louis Armstrong or Lenny Bruce. Second, you can simply be better than anyone else at what you do, like Jimi Hendrix or Eric Clapton. And three is to be unique. No one is ever going to mistake a Bob Dylan record for anything other than a Bob Dylan record, and the same could be said for Joan Armatrading, say, or the Beach Boys. Of the great rappers, Eazy fulfilled that quality of uniqueness.

Two spins of "Boys-N-the-Hood" and I was convinced. I prepared to jettison my whole life and devote myself to this music. If this song was the only one he had, I would devote myself to that one song.

But he didn't have just that one, he had "8 Ball" and "Dopeman," other blood-fresh bulletins from the front lines of the inner city. I couldn't believe it. This guy, this *pisher*, had the goods—the real deal.

"The label you want to start," I asked him, "it have a name?"

"Ruthless Records," he said.

Ruthless. A word from the fourteenth century. Having no "ruth," or pity. "Without rue," meaning without regret. Synonyms: pitiless, callous, inhuman, heartless, cold-blooded, remorseless, implacable, cruel, relentless, severe, ferocious, vicious, cutthroat.

Perfect, I thought. Perfect for the world I was hearing described in those songs.

"And the group?" I asked him. "What do you call them?"

"N.W.A.," he said.

"N.W.A.," I said. "What's that mean, 'No Whites Allowed'?"

That was the first time I heard Eric Wright laugh.

"Sort of," he said. "Close enough."

V

Eric never intended to be a rapper. He saw himself as more of a behind-the-camera kind of guy. He backed into his performance on "Boyz-N-the-Hood" in classic show business manner, like Eve Harrington taking over for Margo Channing in *All About Eve*. The understudy became the star.

It all happened because Dre didn't pay his traffic tickets— didn't pay, and didn't pay, until finally, inevitably in L.A. where young blacks get stopped by the police all the time, he would get hauled off to jail on "failure to appear" beefs. Again and again. He'd use his one phone call to contact Alonzo Williams. And because Lonzo usually needed Dre for some Wreckin' Cru gig, he'd post Andre's bail. Again and again.

Finally Lonzo got sick of it and told Dre that he'd just have to rot in the slammer this time. So Dre called Eazy, and Eazy called me to arrange a bail bondsman. (I was now Eazy's go-to guy, the guy who, if you have a single quarter left to your name, was the one you were going to call.)

"Sure," Eazy told Dre. "I'll post your bail. But you got to do something for me."

It's a time-honored inner-city move, to bail someone out of jail and thereby gain some measure of respect, friendship, or control. Suge Knight signed Tupac to Death Row Records by doing this exact thing, arranging to get Tupac out of jail when he was inside on a sex abuse rap. Come to think of it, my pal Jack Kellman and I once helped facilitate the release of singer Flora Purim—although I didn't strong-arm her into a contract because of it.

In this way, Eazy was owed a favor from Dre. So if you want to follow the twisted logic of the facts, Dre became a superstar because he found himself in jail with no one to post his bail, because the LAPD harassed him, because he ignored his traffic tickets. And Lonzo Williams let the biggest prize in rap music slip away.

Eazy called in his marker. He wanted Dre to lay down some beats for a DJ-style collective he was forming, "N.W.A. and the Posse." Yella could be in it too, Eazy said, and he also recruited Arabian Prince, a smooth, polished producer.

I had heard Arabian Prince's work that first day at Macola, since he was the mixmaster behind the original version of "Supersonic" by the girl rap group J.J. Fad. His real name was Kim Nazel, which he sometimes represented as "Mik Lezan." Nazel was a skinny little guy whose body seemed to be all head. A dapper clotheshorse, he came from a little more upscale background than the rest of the guys in the group. He dressed in tailored suits, drove a nice car, didn't seem to have any money worries.

Another recruit whom Eazy roped in was very young—still in high school, as a matter of fact, when the supergroup was being put together. O'Shea Jackson worked on raps with Dre. He wrote the lyrics to "Boyz-N-the-Hood" in English class. He wrote most of "Dopeman" and "8 Ball," too. That's all O'Shea Jackson did, on his long bus rides north from his home neighborhood in Compton to Taft High School on Ventura Boulevard in the Valley, where he was a cog in the L.A. school district's half-baked integration effort.

O'Shea never went anywhere without his notebook. He wrote in his bedroom in Compton, where his mother, a high-powered, extremely capable woman, encouraged him. He wrote and wrote and wrote. Meanwhile, he became a member of a couple of

Lonzo's minor DJ collectives, the Stereo Cru and C.I.A. It was in C.I.A. that O'Shea Jackson first took his stage name.

Ice Cube.

More than anyone else, Cube popularized the gangsta persona that has come to dominate rap music. There were others who came before. Ice-T's "Six in the Morning" was probably L.A.'s first gangsta rap song, and Philadelphia's Schoolly D recorded street-crime raps on his 1987 album *Saturday Night!* But the scribblings in O'Shea Jackson's school notebooks would eventually form the backbone of a whole new genre.

So the group Eric called N.W.A. and the Posse contained most of the elements necessary to make great rap records. Producers, like Dre and Yella from the Wreckin' Cru, and Arabian Prince. A street poet in the person of O'Shea Jackson, aka Ice Cube. An ever-changing, always-interesting lineup of friends, homies, DJs, and musicians.

But it was Eazy who put it all together. Without Eazy there would be no Dre, no Cube, no N.W.A. I'm not saying those guys would have wound up pumping gas if Eazy hadn't come along and dragooned them into a collective of West Coast rap superstars. But without Eric Wright and Jerry Heller, history would not have happened in the precise way that it did.

What did Eazy bring to the table? Vision, concept, all the big fancy words that people use when they talk about making something happen. Remember where popular music was at that point in time—dominated by Michael Jackson and Prince. Eazy effectively said *That ain't the way to go. This is the way to go.* His vision was complex enough, tight enough, and right enough to attract geniuses such as Dr. Dre and Ice Cube.

Eric's first move was to try to place the songs of his new DJ collective with an established rap group. He rented time at a Torrance recording studio called Audio Achievements, run by an energetic fireplug of a guy named Donovan "Dirtbiker" Smith. From the Roadium to Audio Achievements was maybe five miles as the crow flies. Eazy stuck close to his roots.

Dre, Yella, Arabian Prince, and Eazy assembled at Audio Achievements to present a rough cut of "Boyz-N-the-Hood" to H.B.O., a couple of East Coast rappers. The track didn't even have a vocal laid down—just Dre and Yella's beats and lyrics written in Cube's tattered school notebook.

The forties movie star and tough guy George Raft was famous for turning down roles that other actors, usually Humphrey Bogart, eventually made famous. Raft turned down Sam Spade in *The Maltese Falcon* and Rick in *Casablanca*. Bogart's agent used to sell his client on a role simply by telling him that George Raft had passed on it.

In what surely ranks as an ultimate George Raft moment, the members of H.B.O., in their infinite wisdom, turned down "Boyz-N-the-Hood."

"Too West Coast," they said. Not only that, but they disliked the whole Audio Achievements vibe enough to walk out of the studio—out of the studio and, it turns out, into the mists of history, since H.B.O. vanished from the music scene after the single bad decision for which the group is known.

Unlike Eve Harrington in *All About Eve*, Eazy resisted the call to take over the lead on "Boyz-N-the-Hood." Cube wasn't around, and Dre certainly wasn't going to do it. Eventually, Dre and Yella prevailed upon Eric, and thus was born Eazy-E, West Coast rapper extraordinaire. It was a rocky start. Lonzo recalled a lot of snickering at Macola over the quality of the resulting rap.

Dopeman, dopeman
Hey, man, give me a hit

Eric was very good at deflecting lines of conversation. I eventually came to see him as Machiavellian in his ability to manipulate people. *The Prince* could have been written about Eric Wright. I could not pin him down. If he didn't want to say something, it wouldn't get said.

"You get paid selling drugs?" I asked, trying to push him.

Stone-faced. I waited. He waited.

"I got a money tree in my backyard," he finally said.

I laughed. "You do, huh?" I said. "How do I get me one of those?"

I launched into a meditation on the Racketeer Influenced and Corrupt Organizations Act, the Federal anti-organized-crime measure nicknamed RICO. "What do you do the first time you get a little money?" I asked rhetorically. "You buy your mama a house." With RICO, I told him, you get busted selling drugs, pretty soon Federal agents show up at the front door of your mama's new house, seizure papers in hand.

"You don't want your mama to have a seizure, do you?" I joked, trying to keep the tone light.

Of course, he made no response. Still laughing, I gave up. I've since come to question the whole notion of Eric as a dope dealer. I know that it has become part of the accepted mythology behind the creation of Ruthless: The label was funded in part by dope money. The idea lent us a lot street credibility, so I never bothered to deny it. I mean, given the reputation of Ruthless Records, it *should* have been true.

But I don't think so. I certainly never witnessed Eric sell any coke. I saw him give away a lot of marijuana in his day—he used to keep garbage bags full of pot that were given to him by his street connections, but I never really even saw him sell any of that, either. And I was with him day in and day out over the course of several years.

I think now that the whole "dope dealer" tag was part of Eric Wright's self-forged armor. The hood where he grew up was a dangerous place. He was a small guy. "Thug" was a role that was widely understood on the street; it gave you a certain level of protection in the sense that people hesitated to fuck with you. Likewise, "dope dealer" was a role that accorded you certain privileges and respect.

No one survived on the streets without a protective mask. No one survived naked. You had to have a role. You had to be "thug," "playa," "athlete," "gangsta," or "dope man." Otherwise, there was only one role left to you.

"Victim."

So Eric took on one of the only roles that allowed him to operate. Was it for real? I didn't think so, and no one else who was really close to him thought so either. But it's become an unchallengeable part of the Eazy-E mythology.

Far be it from me to dispel such an effective bit of mythology. I will say that the first $250,000 slugged into Ruthless Records was mine, and that I put up another million over the first few years of the label's existence. I thus went against the sage advice of one of the smartest men I have ever met, David Geffen, whose business mantra was always "OPM"—other people's money. David made an art of using OPM to start his businesses.

When Eazy didn't want to talk about something, he'd

suddenly go off on an entirely new tangent, usually one that he chose because he knew it would be extra enticing to you. That's what happened that first day at Macola, when I was trying to extract information about his dope-dealing past.

"I want to go into business with you, man," he said, switching subjects abruptly. "We could do everything fifty-fifty, half and half, down the middle. You own half the label and I own half."

"Half-ownership? Why would you want to do that?"

"Well, I figure it would make the math real simple."

I laughed again. I was starting to like him.

"Don't worry about the math," I said. "I've been in the business a long time. I can do the percentages in my head."

"Yeah?" he said, immediately challenging me. "Okay, give me twelve percent of thirty-eight K."

"Fuck you," I said. "I don't work for twelve percent."

"I knew it was bullshit."

I said, "Four thousand, five-sixty, okay?" I grew up in the era before calculators. The bookies and gamblers that I came up with could all do numbers in their head. If I don't nail the percentage exactly, I'll be close enough that you'll think I'm right anyway.

"No calculator, man!" he said, impressed.

"Here's the thing, Eric," I said. "That fifty-fifty deal is real generous, but this has got to be all yours. Ruthless Records has got to be Eric Wright, sole owner and proprietor."

He thought about that. "How you going to get paid?" he asked.

"Every dollar comes into Ruthless, I take twenty cents. That's industry standard for a manager of my caliber. I take twenty, you take eighty percent. I am responsible for my expenses, and you're responsible for yours. You own the company. I work for you."

I could tell he liked my deal a lot better than the one he had proposed. He hesitated, though, trying to figure the logic behind someone negotiating downward.

I laid it out to him. "Total black ownership, one hundred percent. It doesn't make any sense any other way."

I believed it back then, and I still believe now that it was the right path to take. Ruthless was Eric Wright's initiative, his concept, his creation. He even came up with the name.

What was I going to do, ride in on him like Colonel Parker rode in on Elvis, grabbing 50 percent? Those days were long gone. (In the Colonel's defense, his was the most successful artist-manager team in history, and he had only one client.) At that point in my career, I earned the commission of all top managers, which was 20 percent. In fact, I was known as "H20," meaning Heller at 20 percent.

I also quite consciously grappled with the fact that I was a Jewish male and he was an African-American male. History had loaded that particular dynamic with plenty of freight. I wanted to bend over backward to do what was right. And I think I did. Later on people used this deal to discredit me, but it definitely fit within the industry standards for a start-up act. And the truth was that Eric would have gladly paid me 80 percent.

My first meeting with Eric was one of the great three-hour periods of my life. I didn't have to take a few days to think about it, and neither did he. We both just *knew*. When we entered that room, Ruthless was just an idea, a phantasm, a collection of neuroelectrical impulses firing in Eric Wright's brain. There were no Ruthless artists, no Ruthless offices, no Ruthless logo. Nothing.

But when we left the conference room that afternoon, Ruthless was real, as real as Warner Brothers, Elektra, or Atlantic. We were in business.

VI

RESTAURANTS I HAVE KNOWN AND LOVED: PART ONE

Restaurants are the life-blood of the music business, just as much as they are the life-blood of Hollywood and Wall Street and Washington. The restaurant world is like an alternative reality. It's alive. It glitters. It removes you from the mundane.

Part of my job as an agent is to know the great restaurants in any town I find myself, but most particularly in my home town of Los Angeles. Not only that, but I have to know how to get the right table at those restaurants. To a lesser extent, I have to know hotels, car dealerships, liquor stores, cigar shops, and—in times past—drug dealers. Hey, music management is a service industry.

I've known and loved Martoni's restaurant almost as long as I've been in L.A. It was, not to put too fine a point on it, a mob-frequented place, a long-time Sinatra favorite. But it was also a music industry hangout, where Jerry Moss and Herbie Alpert met up before they founded A&M Records. Martoni's was an old-style refuge. I used to call it the "dinner sanctum." The lights of L.A. rolled out below you, the freeways pulsed and flowed, but you were above it all, unreachable and immune.

As soon as I shook hands with Eric Wright and left Macola that afternoon in March 1987, I immediately began calling every artist who I was representing back then. I either spoke or left messages with each one.

I told them all the same thing. Meet me in the back room at Martoni's tomorrow afternoon.

Most of them showed. Morey was at my side. Rudy Pardee and his partner on the Dream Team. A rap duo who called themselves Rodney O & Joe Cooley. Arabian Prince. A soulful heavy-breather who went by the name of Egyptian Lover. Alonzo Williams and most of the members of the World Class Wreckin' Cru. Russ Parr, who had a band known as Bobby Jimmy and the Critters. A guy I didn't even manage who went by the handle of the Unknown DJ. There were many more, and they were all gathered at Martoni's.

I stood up to address them.

"I've been representing all of you, and we've been doing good business together. But I'd like to let you know there's been a change in my status," I said. "As of yesterday I became general manager in Ruthless Records, which is wholly owned by Eric Wright."

I gave a nod in Eazy's direction. I explained that the two of us had gone into business the day before, and that this meeting would serve as their notice for a shift in my approach.

"That's right, that's right, now comes the bad news," piped up the Unknown DJ, aka Andre Manuel. I couldn't believe it. I was being heckled by a guy who wasn't even signed with me. The Unknown DJ's father had been a Muslim, and I sometimes wonder if he made my life miserable just on principle, just because in his eyes I was a honky motherfucker.

I soldiered on despite the heckling.

"I will no longer be representing anyone who is not signed to Ruthless Records," I explained. "Those of you who don't wish to sign with us, that's perfectly okay. I'll help you secure other representation. Those of you who do want to become artists on Ruthless, I will continue to manage and promote your careers, but we will now have a record label that we can call home."

Eazy made no speech. As usual, he said nothing at all.

Looking back, the announcement demonstrates the extremity of my response to meeting Eric Wright. I had never laid eyes on him before Tuesday, March 3, 1987. On Wednesday, the very next afternoon, I stood up in front of my whole client list and publicly threw my lot in with Ruthless. At that point in time, the label was simply a handshake between the two of us. Nothing better illustrates Eric Wright's personal charisma, the intensity of his purpose, or the power of his personality, than the fact that I performed this all-or-nothing leap on the basis of a handshake.

Some of the artists I spoke to that day signed with Ruthless. Some of them didn't. It didn't matter to me. I did not look back. I might have had a thought—*Jesus, now I have to make this work*—but I recall very clearly liking the fact I had made a leap without knowing precisely where I was going to land.

That night, Eric and I stayed on at Martoni's for dinner after the others left. We had a lot to talk about. He never drank alcohol that much, but as the evening wore on he had a couple Midori sours. I was drinking my usual, ice-cold Russian vodka. We may have toasted to Ruthless once or twice. I don't remember.

But I do recall that the future looked pretty bright to me, especially after my third or fourth vodka. I think it looked bright to Eric, too, because he seemed happy and at ease. There was no apparent reason for optimism, given the current state of East Coast-dominated rap music, the low rate of success for music start-ups, and the bargain-basement basis of our beginnings. But we were optimistic nonetheless.

We couldn't have known that it was going to be a short run, and that eight years later to the month he would be dead.

THE DAYZ OF WAYBACK

The negotiation is the hardest part

I

Cleveland in August 1945, the weekend after V-J Day.
Outside it was a sweltering, humid summer morning, with the
locusts just cranking up in the elms. "Hundred-hundreds" we
used to call them—100-degree heat, 100 percent humidity.

But inside the Kibitzer's Club was cool and dark. People were
still high from the war ending. I was a child of four sitting atop an
old-style Coca-Cola cooler in a gambling den at ten a.m. on a
Saturday. I could see my father down the smoky hallway, checking
the odds on the tote board. The huge blackboard in the card room
listed all the day's games, a skell writing and erasing them with
chalk and a wet rag.

I kicked my heels against the red-enameled sheet metal of the
cooler and drew the attention of Alex "Shondor" Birns, a tough-
as-nails Hungarian Jew who looked like an eight-foot guy hammered into a five-foot-eight mold, all muscle and bone-hard
facial angles. "Shondor the Bull," they called him.

Hilda and Dave Heller

For some reason, I wasn't afraid of him, and I think he saw that, and it pleased him.

"You're Davey's kid, aren't you?" he asked in European-accented English. "You going to be a high roller like your old man when you grow up?"

"I'm already a high roller," I said.

He laughed. "Sure you are," he said. "How old are you?"

"Five," I lied. It was almost true. Another couple of months.

"I'll give you a piece of advice, kid. Always keep to the outside."

He bobbed and weaved in place like a fullback. He was telling me to stay clear of the crowd, find your own way, go where the other guy ain't.

"All right, kid? You're gonna do that for me? Stay to the outside?"

I solemnly said that I would.

I'm not sure what the Cleveland gangster Shondor Birns would have made of Eazy-E and *Straight Outta Compton*. I like to think he would have understood and approved if he had it all properly translated for him—*mutatis mutandis*, as the Latin phrase goes, "with proper changes made." Shondor, the toughest Jew who ever lived, was a looming figure of my youth in Cleveland, Ohio. A top-level boss in the Cleveland syndicate, he had embarked on his criminal career way back in the 1920s with payroll robbery, before graduating to bootlegging and the numbers racket.

Over the years and in the course of countless crimes, and despite being labeled Cleveland's public enemy number one, the Bull magically dodged jail again and again. It wasn't for lack of trying. Shondor once dumped a World War II hand grenade into the backseat of an unoccupied police car, blowing its roof off. Fuck tha police, indeed.

Eventually, Shondor Birns wound up hoisted by his own petard, blown to bits himself by parties unknown. Whoever did the job wanted to make sure. They found pieces of the Bull's body six blocks away. But when I knew him, he was still intact, the king of the Cleveland numbers racket, owning the bookie joint my father took me to as a child, every Saturday morning like clockwork.

Gangsta, gangsta.

I thought of Shondor Birns driving home from Martoni's the night after performing my no-net swan dive into the world of Ruthless Records. He was my touchstone, probably the first gangster I ever met.

I thought about Shondor and about growing up in the Cleveland of my youth, and how it had set me up to deal with what was coming at me, straight out of Compton.

I used to play my Cleveland-raised mother the hard-core hip-hop cuts from Macola Records. She'd listen and pretend that she didn't hear the cussing. She loved the music because she loved Eazy, and she loved Eazy because of what he did for me. But her tastes ran more to Frank Sinatra and Tony Bennett.

Back when I was living at my parents' house, I used to be woken up every morning by the sound of my seventy-year-old father lifting weights. Dave Heller always engaged his existence like a wrestler engages his opponent. He was born on Friday the thirteenth in the thirteenth year of the last century—at thirteen minutes to three, if you want to get supernatural about it. If there were a thirteenth month to get born in, he would have probably done that, too, but as it was he had to settle for June.

His father, my grandfather, broke the mold of the bookish Jewish scholar to become one of the standout athletes in Ohio of the early 1900s. Pete Heller played semipro football against one of the greatest athletes of all time, Jim Thorpe. He also played baseball with Honus Wagner, whose baseball card is the most valuable in existence.

To duck under the rigid norms of Jewish respectability, Pete Heller always used an assumed name, Pete Southern, when he played sports. Working as a professional athlete was a *shanda*, a disgrace. But there he is, barrel-chested and fierce, enshrined in the Jewish Sports Hall of Fame. (Yes, there is such a thing as a Jewish Sports Hall of Fame.)

Pete Heller, aka Pete Southern, lost his white-metal business in the Depression. He retired from athletics to work for dapper little bow-tied Jo Tyroler, overseeing the blast furnaces at Tyroler Metals. Pete would take me down to the foundry early on bone-cold Cleveland mornings. His foreman, a huge black man named CJ, was one of his best friends. CJ would ignite the furnaces and pitch in shovelfuls of bituminous coal. I felt the sudden suck of air as the blast furnaces started to burn, making a sound like a rocket engine. Then the cherry-red molten metal poured down the feeder trench into ingot molds. For a five-year-old, it was the best spectacle imaginable.

We'd watch CJ light the furnaces and then Pete would say, "Let's go down to Plant X."

Tyroler had a lot of different plants, Plant A, Plant B, Plant C, but "Plant X" was a no-name tavern up the street, in the nastiest part of town, the all-Polish west side. Pete would stroll in and lift his little-tyke grandson onto the bar. He didn't need to order. The bartender knew what he wanted.

"Don't tell mama," Pete said as he was served a huge schooner of beer in a heavyweight glass. I couldn't lift it. Most guys drank a schooner with two hands. My grandfather would take a double shot of whiskey and drop it, shot-glass and all, straight down into the schooner. A boilermaker. The breakfast of champions.

Pete was always a big drinker, especially after his business went bust. When I was six or seven, I scraped up my savings and bought him a bottle of top-of-the-line Canadian whiskey, Seagram's V.O., the Bronfman family's prestige brand. He was knocked out by the gesture, but the next day, he drew me aside.

"You know, Gerala, this stuff is wasted on me," he said, caressing the amber-colored bottle of V.O. "For the price of this I could get three bottles of Old Crow. Would you mind if I go down to the liquor store and made a trade?"

I laughed and said that of course I didn't mind.

My father grew up smoothly handsome, square-jawed and big, just like my grandfather. Dave Heller came out of Glenville High School and landed straight in the poverty-stricken lap of the Great Depression. He followed his father Pete into the trade of buying and selling scrap white metal, lead, tungsten, nickel, tin, pewter.

I've always wondered what kind of scrappiness it took to enter the scrap metal business at the tail end of the Great Depression, but whatever brand it was, my father had it. He operated on the time-honored principle that if you can buy something for one dollar, and sell it to someone else for two dollars, you had a living.

He managed not only to survive, but prosper. In 1938, he married my mother Hilda Kaufman, who he met because her five brothers kept a fruit-and-vegetable stand near the temple the Hellers attended—or rather, in Dave's case, didn't attend, because my father could never be described as an observant Jew. He laid eyes on the Torah maybe two or three times a year, on high holy days only.

My father's real milieu was not temple, not his home life with my mother and me, not even his scrap metal business. Like a lot of the married men of his day, he spent a majority of his time away from home, inhabiting the world of fraternal clubs, booze-heavy chophouses, and members-only gambling joints. He moved easily through the demimonde, which in Cleveland at that time—post-Prohibition, mid-Depression—was mobbed up within an inch of its life.

The story of organized crime in Cleveland could provide abundant material for a gangsta rap album. Though the city never enjoyed the criminal reputation of Chicago, say, or New York City, its history is certainly bloody enough.

Cleveland's mob was built on corn sugar, one of the prime ingredients for corn liquor, and on geography. During the Prohibition era, Lake Erie and the Detroit River became vast, very busy Broadways for bootleggers. Smugglers extraordinaire Samuel Bronfman—yes, he of the Seagram fortune—and Joseph Kennedy—yes, he of the son in the White House—would load up the three-hundred-horsepower tugs of the "Big Jewish Navy" in Canada, speed over the river or across the choppy waters of the lake, and unload at the foot of Mayfield Road in Cleveland.

Waiting there to pick up the hooch were the trucks of Morris Barney Dalitz, originally a Detroit boy with ties to the Purple Gang, but now ensconced as the Godfather of the infamous Mayfield Road Mob.

Moe Dalitz always put up a bland, avuncular front. When

summoned to Senator Estes Kefauver's organized crime hearings, he patiently explained, "If you people wouldn't have drunk it, I wouldn't have bootlegged it." He had a point.

But behind the unassuming exterior, Dalitz was a gangster's gangster. He was friendly with the crème de la capos: Bugsy Siegel, Frank Costello, Meyer Lansky. He attended the bon voyage party when Lucky Luciano was deported by the C.I.A. in order to help clear Italy of the fascist menace and kick off the French Connection. My father didn't exactly move in Moe's rarefied circles, but he knew Dalitz and the syndicate boys well enough, simply by virtue of swimming in the same murky Cleveland waters as they did.

That was the world I was born into, on October 6, 1940, at Cleveland's Mount Sinai Hospital. I would grow up to call Moe Dalitz "Uncle Moe." I saw him all the time; he lived around the corner from us. My dad wasn't a gangster and he wasn't a criminal, but he sure liked to rub padded shoulders with them. He was a high roller, interested in nightlife, horses, organized athletics, dice, bookies, touts, and card games.

But Shondor the Bull Birns, the guy I first met that weekend after V-J Day at Kibitzer's, was my real gangster godfather. He was a bigger-than-life figure to me, even though he was a rung below people like Moe Dalitz on the mob ladder. After that first Coke-cooler meeting, we got to know each other, and over time, we struck up an understanding.

I wouldn't exactly characterize it as a friendship, more like a collegial relationship. I'd pretend to be older than I was and he would pretend to take me seriously. I'd sit on the Coke cooler while my dad bet Ohio State–Michigan and Shondor would advise me on the realities of life.

"You are now about to witness the strength of street knowledge." I think Shondor the Bull would have used that expression had he thought of it first.

Even though my mother was a fabulous cook, my family ate out almost every night, making the rounds of mob-hangout restaurants on an unalterable weekly schedule. Tuesdays it was the Theatrical Grill, run by Mushy Wexler. Wednesdays was always the Zephyr Room, owned by Morris Kleinman of the syndicate. Thursdays was the Hickory Grill, a mock-Tudor place that boasted about its liver and bacon entrée and French fried frogs legs.

Friday was the big night at the Alhambra, a place owned by Shondor himself, downstairs next to a bowling alley. Saturdays we went to Kornmans, owned by Billy Weinberger, who went on to be the president of Caesars Palace and then the head of Resorts International.

Wartime prosperity and then the postwar boom lifted the Heller family up through the social strata as though we were flying on a magic carpet. I began my life in the Glenville, not exactly a ghetto by European standards but a low-rent neighborhood all the same. Cleveland wasn't a melting pot. Poles stayed with Poles, Irish with Irish, and the Jews stayed in the Glenville. When you walked through the Polish west-side neighborhoods, they'd shout questions at you in Polish. If you couldn't understand, they knew you weren't one of them, and you got your ass kicked.

As the scrap metal business took off, we decamped for successively tonier neighborhoods, first to Cleveland Heights and then, in 1948, to the real home turf of my youth, Shaker Heights. Eazy had his Compton, I had my Shaker Heights. Moving on up, as the *Jeffersons* theme song used to say.

I was befuddled. "What's going on?"

The officer with Yella, a red-faced guy with a shaggy mustache, glanced over at me with mild curiosity, then went back to his business. He had Yella kneeling up against the stucco front of Audio Achievements.

Eazy said, "Jerry, hey, just chill."

Which drew a nudging kick from the second cop, spreading Eazy's legs apart as the cop forced him against the building too.

"Will someone tell me what's going on?" I said.

But it was as though I were invisible. No one paid me the least bit of attention, although I was standing right there in their midst. I got the idea I was watching some sort of complicated pas de deux, an oft-performed dance to which I didn't know the steps. The cops stripped the wallets from their quarry, checking their IDs and then dropping the cards and wallets to the pavement.

I knew in theory that this kind of thing had happened to Eazy and the others before, many times, but I had never witnessed it up close. I was getting a taste of Compton reality.

Without apology or explanation, the officers turned heel, got back in their squad car and drove leisurely away.

"What the hell was that?" I asked. Eazy and the others didn't seem to think it was any big deal.

"Day in the life," Dre said.

None of them seemed too eager to give the time of day to the white guy in a suit in their midst—not right at that moment in time.

"Fuck it, Jerry," Eazy said.

"Fuck what?" I said. "You mean, 'Fuck you, Jerry'? I didn't do anything."

"Just fuck it," he said. "I'm tired." He and the others ducked back into the studio.

I've always thought back to that afternoon in the wake of the squalls of outrage that greeted N.W.A.'s incendiary music. Right, right, I would think. Young African-American males put up with a constant, grinding campaign of humiliation and harassment from the day they hit puberty, sometimes before. Day after day, they are proned out, yanked from their cars, hassled, beaten, and all too often murdered.

Assume the position, motherfuckers.

Then a group of twenty-year-olds has the stones, the absolute audacity to raise a brash voice of complaint. And *they* are the ones who get criticized and threatened? The members of N.W.A. are the ones called out on the carpet for their "attitude"? They make a *record* and you complain? Where were the self-righteous blowhards when Dr. Dre, perhaps the premier musical genius of our day, was getting forced to his knees on the hot sidewalks of Torrance? (Or Compton, or Norwalk, or Inglewood . . .)

It's Newton's Third Law again: For every action there is an equal and opposite reaction. Where did all of N.W.A.'s attitude come from? Do you really have to look any further than the relentless, unending crusade in this country against the young African-American male, by American society as a whole and by Los Angeles–area police in particular?

Policing in Los Angeles is conducted on a whole different level from other places. Los Angeles sprawls over 465 square miles, and the LAPD has a paltry 8,400 officers to patrol it with. (The NYPD, by contrast, employs 39,110 officers to cover 321 square miles.) How does such a small force as the

LAPD maintain control in such a geographically massive city as Los Angeles?

By being the meanest, ass-kickingest motherfuckers in town, that's how. Here's the unofficial credo of the LAPD, as interpreted by writer and LAPD chronicler Joe Domanick: "Give no slack and take no shit from anyone. Confront and command. Control the streets at all times. Always be aggressive. Stop crimes before they happen. Seek them out. Shake them down. Make the arrest. And never, never admit that the department did anything wrong."

Or how about getting it straight from the horse's mouth, from then-LAPD Police Chief Daryl Gates's testimony before the U.S. Senate? "Casual drug users," said Gates, "should be taken out and shot."

Oftentimes, in the Los Angeles of the 1980s under the iron fist of Daryl Gates, casual drug users *were* shot—them, and also quite a few innocent bystanders whose skin happened to be brown.

Every time I saw the military buzz cut of Daryl Gates on television the word "nimrod" would bubble up as an unbidden reaction. Daryl started out his career as the driver for the previous chief of police, William Parker, another total buzz-cut squareball. He's the namesake of LAPD's downtown headquarters, the Parker Center, and the real guy was just as square and ugly as the building.

Even though he was a sullen alcoholic, Bill Parker managed to put up such a straight arrow facade that a one-time LAPD officer named Gene Roddenberry modeled his *Star Trek* character of Spock after him. Parker also inspired the clipped, "just the facts" speech of Jack Webb on the TV show *Dragnet*.

Together, Parker and his protégé Gates presided over a police department that to many onlookers was engaged in a pogrom against the non-white citizenry of Los Angeles.

To protect and serve . . . yeah, protect their own asses and serve up a whole lot of ass-whupping to whomever crosses their paths. LAPD officers routinely refer to the force as "the biggest, baddest gang in L.A."

Eazy, Dre, and Cube came of age under this Parker-Gates reign of terror. The soundtrack of their days in South Central was the choppy staccato of the LAPD's Bell Jet Ranger and Aerospatiale helicopters, hovering over their homes and illuminating their backyards with the harsh white glare of halogen spotlights. The rapper Toddy Tee had a huge hit with "Batterram," describing a machine of terror that was much beloved by Daryl Gates.

Could I blame Eazy for a little attitude? Not at all. In fact, when I got to know him better, I was most impressed with his ultimate forbearance. He had been hassled by police his whole life. I wasn't at all surprised he was pissed. But I was amazed and impressed that he hadn't acted out his angry impulses. He hadn't gone ahead and, in the language of the hood, "wetted up" a few cops.

Except on his records, of course, where he killed quite a few.

II

The seething anger of Eazy-E powered the recording

sessions at Audio Achievements over the summer and fall of 1987.

"All we're doing, we're plugging into Eric's life," Dre told me once when I dropped by the sound studio. I got an image of a finger jammed into a light socket.

While *N.W.A. and the Posse* had been the product of a loose amalgamation of DJs, musicians and MCs, around this time the group's lineup became more well-defined. N.W.A. coalesced around Eazy-E, Dr. Dre, and Ice Cube, with DJ Yella and Arabian Prince taking auxiliary roles.

"I was the conceptualizer, Ice Cube was the lyricizer, and Dre was the musicalizer," Eazy used to tell journalists. (Which made me, I guess, the financializer.)

N.W.A. was Eazy's concept. He charted the direction that the group took. He was the socket they plugged into. That was his genius.

No compromises, no nods to civility, no bows to polite discourse, just raw portraits of the sights, sounds, and situations he saw around him—street knowledge, undistilled. Other labels could censor and shape their artists. At Ruthless, the goal was to put the real thing across, unfiltered.

It was as though Eazy were saying to the world, "You gonna shove me into a corner? Okay, here is what my corner looks like."

Eazy and Dre had their own chemistry. Eazy freed Dre to be who he really wanted to be. As sick as he was of the Wreckin' Cru's lavender jumpsuits, he was even sicker of Lonzo's Temptations stylings. He didn't want to scratch his turntables to

Lonzo's ballads. Eazy offered Dre a chance to create from the gritty world they both moved in, not from some fantasy world of sequins and lace.

"I make music for my friends to listen to," Eazy said. And that's what Dre wanted too.

As the sessions that produced tracks for the albums *Eazy-Duz-It* and *Straight Outta Compton* continued, I became increasingly awed by Andre Young's work ethic. The guy was a demon. Propped up on a rolling chair in front of the Audio Achievements mixing board, Dre worked for four, six, eight, sometimes twelve hours straight, sending out for food, rarely leaving the board.

If I came into the control room during a recording session and didn't see Dre in his chair, I simply waited a beat. There was a door to a bathroom at the opposite end of the room and, inevitably, Dre would emerge from that door and sit back down at the mixing board. The board or the bathroom: the only two places you would find him.

Technology made Dre. Dirtbiker Smith taught him a lot, but like all genius students, Dre quickly outstripped his teacher. Dre got influenced by a lot of people. He was a sponge. Eventually he started doing his own mixes. He was the first world-class artist to come of age in the era of the sound sample, when songs were not so much played or created as visualized and constructed. He wasn't a great instrumentalist. He played some keyboards, that's all.

Dre's partner in High Powered Productions was Yella, who usually sat in front of Dre, next to the couch in the control room. Yella was always the drum machine guy. The two had a spooky, psychic connection. With Yella on the drum machine, Dre

Andre Young, aka Dr. Dre, the reigning musical genius of our age, with his then-girlfriend, the Ruthless R&B sensation Michelle Toussaint, aka Michel'le

professional relationship, and I sensed Joe Smith had taken a genuine liking to me over the years.

Capitol was a natural place for N.W.A.—one of the big kids on the block, with a lot of distribution muscle behind it. Al Teller at Columbia had just made a deal with Def Jam, Russell Simmons and Rick Rubin's seminal East Coast label, and MCA had Run-D.M.C.'s Profile Records under its distribution umbrella. Capitol needed a presence in rap. I knew it, and Joe Smith knew it too.

So I brought Joe Smith the greatest rap music I ever heard, N.W.A. Smith was always impeccably groomed and dressed. One of the true gentlemen of the business. We sat in his office in the old Capitol building, the round tower near Hollywood and Vine that was supposed to resemble a stack of forty-five-rpm singles.

I played him "Boyz-N-the-Hood." A cloud passed across the True Gentleman's face. I knew I was in trouble.

"Here," I said, flipping the N.W.A. demo tape over on the gazillion-dollar sound system he had in his office. "This is killer."

I played him "Dopeman."

"Stop, stop!" the True Gentleman said, as Eazy barreled into the chorus.

Dopeman, dopeman
Well, suck this, bitch

Silence in the room. The True Gentleman had a pained look on his face, as though I had just stunk up his office.

"Jerry," he began, and right then, just by the tone of his

voice, I knew that I had lost him. *The bet is won or lost before you tee off.* "What makes you think anyone is going to buy this garbage? Who's going to listen? Tell me who is going to play it? No radio station in the world."

In Joe Smith's mind, promotion was all about getting records on the radio. He started out as a disc jockey in Boston. If he couldn't get it on the radio, he couldn't sell it.

"Joe, listen to me," I said, improvising as well as I could. "Remember when we came up in the business, nobody would play 'Let's Spend the Night Together' by the Rolling Stones? Even FM wouldn't touch it. The boys went on Ed Sullivan, they had to sing it, 'Let's spend some *time* together.' Now the song's on classic rock stations, no one bats an eye. Today Mick Jagger is Frank Sinatra. Times change. In ten years, N.W.A. will be all over the place."

"Never," Joe Smith said. "This crap is never going to make it."

"Joe, it's the Black Panthers. It's the fucking Rolling Stones."

"I'll tell you what I'll do, Jerry," he said. "I'll pay you right now, today, one million dollars for the rights to the name of Ruthless Records. It's a great name. Really, I'll have my girl bring in the checkbook."

He raised his voice to show he was not kidding. "Suzy!"

"I don't want to sell the name. I want to sell the music."

"Never," the True Gentleman said. "It'll never go."

Suzy came in. As in most businesses, in music the secretaries are always much prettier than the executives.

"Forget it, Suzy," Joe said. "He doesn't have anything to sell. He's crazy. Jerry Heller has officially gone crazy."

After getting enough doors slammed in my face, I was having doubts about my sanity myself. Columbia, SLAM! Capitol,

SLAM! Elektra, SLAM! Atlantic, SLAM! I knocked on a dozen doors, and got nine turn-downs. The other three labels stopped taking my calls.

"That's cool," Eric said, when I relayed Joe Smith's reaction. "Fuck 'em. What we do is concentrate on our girls."

When Eazy said "concentrate on our girls" he didn't mean "pussy." (If he meant "pussy," he would have said "bitches.") He meant the early female rap act, J.J. Fad, who had signed to Ruthless.

We were sitting in the first corporate offices of Ruthless Records on Strathern Street in Canoga Park. Nearby was Lanark Park, a four-block square city green space that was, in those days, something of a drug bazaar. I recall going to work one morning and seeing the bodies of gangbangers who had been chained to trees in the park and shot by a rival gang.

The neighborhood hosted industrial parks, loading docks, factories. We shared our office space with my brother's *Los Angeles Times* distributorship, which he ran at night. The place was shabby and claustrophobic, a first-floor suite with offices in the front formerly used by Caballero Films, one of the leading porn video companies of the day. We used to find old dusty video packaging from their porn films behind all the furniture. Maybe that's where Yella got the idea of going into porn producing on his own.

Our only office amenity back then was a huge Sony Trinitron and a VHS player. Eazy liked to watch Abel Ferrara's great mob movie, *King of New York*, over and over again, twenty-four hours a day. It used to drive me insane.

We got so we could quote the dialogue to each other. He'd crack me up in business meetings by whispering Christopher

Walken's famous line from the movie, "A nickel bag gets sold in the park, I want in."

Whenever Eazy bitched at me, I'd say, channeling Walken's Frank White: "I'm not your problem. I'm a business man." And before Eazy blew off a pistol, he always liked to say, "They're for bullet holes, bitch!" imitating Laurence Fishburne as Jimmy Jump in the scene where he passes off a suitcase full of tampons as cocaine.

King of New York is a modern-day updating of the Robin Hood story. Frank White comes out of prison and takes over his old drug turf, but with a twist. He distributes all the profits to the poor. I think it was Eazy's favorite movie because he saw himself as a sort of Robin Hood. He was always a real easy touch, no pun, when anyone asked a favor, for money, for a demo tape to be played. He was as generous as Elvis. I know he gave away pounds of weed. He saw pot as a way to grease the wheels of business.

It turned out to be a good idea to have located Ruthless offices far from Eric's stomping grounds in South Central. It made it more difficult for hangers-on and wannabes to drop by and interrupt our day. We needed a sanctuary.

The name J.J. Fad represented an abbreviation of the original member's initials. Eventually Eazy decided it should stand for "Just Jammin' Fresh and Def." Juana Burns went by the stage name of M.C.J.B., Dania Birks was Baby-D, and Michelle Franklin became Sassy C. Eazy thought it was important that Ruthless have an act of female rappers. Eazy's instincts were, as usual, right on the money. An East Coast female rap duo called Salt-N-Pepa broke huge nationally that year with a remixed version of their locally released record "Push It." Thus we were in perfect position to pitch J.J. Fad to the labels.

V

One of the more surreal ironies of N.W.A. is that an animated cartoon of dried fruit singing classic soul sponsored by an agricultural association finally opened the door for the World's Most Dangerous Band. You can't get stranger than that on the planet Earth.

Bryan Turner came out of K-tel Entertainment, the packaging and marketing company famous (or infamous) for its line of compilation albums advertised on late-night TV ("Roots of Soul," "Motown Love Collection," "20 Electrifying Hits!" "20 Explosive Hits!" "20 Dynamic Hits!").

K-tel compilations usually had exclamation points behind them. The company was essentially a bottom-feeder. It gobbled up repackaging rights for old songs, manufactured the albums cheaply, and advertised the hell out of them to insomniacs and shut-ins. If you can buy something for a dollar, and sell it for two dollars, you've got a living. K-tel did phenomenally well.

So when Turner left K-tel and formed Priority Records with his partner Mark Cerami, the two of them didn't try to reinvent the wheel. Duplicating the K-tel business model, they issued a couple of rap compilation albums that sold well.

Then Priority hit pay-dirt. The California Raisin Advisory Board, representing a Fresno-based cooperative of raisin growers (actually, of course, they grew grapes, which they then dried to make raisins) put out an ad campaign that featured a group of lovable Claymation raisins singing Marvin Gaye's "I Heard It Through the Grapevine." Academy Award–winning director Will Vinton did the initial 1987 TV commercial.

The American public went nuts for the California Raisins. It turned out the raisins had names (Stretch, Beebop, A.C., and

Red). Eventually, they had TV specials and a Saturday morning cartoon, as well as T-shirts, coffee mugs, action figures, and other merchandise.

And they had a two-million-selling hit album on Priority Records, entitled, tantalizingly and imaginatively enough, *California Raisins Sing the Hit Songs*, on which the dried fruit sang Motown classics by top-echelon songwriters such as Lieber and Stoller, Holland and Dozier, and Otis Redding. Having left Jimi Hendrix's Band of Gypsys, Buddy Miles went on to even greater commercial glory as the lead singer of the California Raisins. I thought the Raisins did a credible version of "When a Man Loves a Woman."

The Raisins were a tough act to follow, but I was desperate. Priority was distributed by Cema, the independent distribution arm of Capitol Records. Capitol had already passed on N.W.A. But everybody in town had turned us down. I made an appointment for me and Eazy to see Bryan Turner at Priority.

I became acquainted with Turner and his business partner Mark Cerami when I had offices on the same floor as K-tel in the Jolly Roger building at Sunset and Cahuenga. The place was named for the street-level coffee shop with the worst food on the face of the planet. The Jolly Roger building was a music industry joint, with tenants such as BMI, Otis Smith's Beverly Glen Music, Seals & Croft, and CNN.

Luck smiled. Just before Eazy and I took our meeting at Priority's Jolly Roger offices, Johnny Phillips of Select-O-Hits, a prime distributor for the label, put in a call to Turner. Phillips raved about Macola's twelve-inch of "Boyz-N-the-Hood." The record, he told Turner, was moving thousands of units. We couldn't have asked for a better testimonial. Eazy of the audience had felt the heavy hand of the LAPD come down on them. When Cube hit the chorus, the crowd unleashed their pain and anger into a deafening unison chant.

Fuck tha police, fuck, fuck, fuck tha police . . .

Bryan Turner might not have believed in the music, but he believed in me. A week after that concert, he and Mark Cerami signed Ruthless to a production deal to release *Straight Outta Compton* and *Eazy-Duz-It* on Priority. Both albums would ship via Cema's national distribution network with the Ruthless logo on them. It was the best of both worlds: major-label clout with effective indie distribution.

Eazy-Duz-It went platinum and sold 2.5 million units. *Straight Outta Compton* went platinum, sold three million records, and transformed hip-hop forever.

VI

When you get swept into a whirlwind you tend to lose perspective. There's no time to take a step back and analyze your next moves. It's not like Dorothy, calmly looking out the window of Auntie Em's house as it wings its way toward Oz, waving at a couple of mooks going by in a rowboat. You don't have time to wave. You're too busy being buffeted.

I don't know about twisters or whirlwinds, but I do know about the steady spiral of intensity that happened in our lives when N.W.A. took off. By the spring of 1989, I couldn't go anywhere south of the 10 freeway without hearing *Straight Outta Compton* on car stereos, from boomboxes, and out of project-housing windows. It hadn't gotten to that point in the Valley quite yet, but I knew it would. Pop culture is a virus. Every time I would telephone someone, I'd hear it playing it the background.

The cell phone was just gaining popularity, and it helped spread the word. Fans would call each other from their cars and say, "Listen to this!" They'd hold up their cell phones to their car stereo speakers, and N.W.A. would get passed on in a crude form of technological tag.

The virus was spreading beyond L.A., too. I flew with Eazy to New York for a music industry function, and while we were there, we got invited to a Bill Graham party at the Park Lane Hotel. The party turned out to be crowded and not much fun. Eazy and I rode down on the elevator afterward. Chaka Khan and Diana Ross were in the same elevator with us. Then three big African-American guys got on. We all crowded together as the elevator started down to the hotel lobby.

The three guys checked out Eazy, nudged each other, and

started laughing. I bristled. Was there going to be a problem here?

Then they began to rap softly.

'Cause the boys in the hood are always hard
You come talkin' that trash, we'll pull ya card

The three guys knew all the words. They did the whole chorus while we plummeted downward to the lobby. I couldn't believe it. Suddenly I realized who they were. Joey Simmons, Jason Mizell, and Darryl McDaniels of Run-D.M.C. At that moment, I knew we were golden. They were exactly the kind of tastemakers to whom I had been tirelessly sending N.W.A. tapes, jackets, and posters. The record wasn't even out yet.

"You know who that was?" I asked Eazy as we stepped off the elevator.

"Sure," he said. Nothing more. Cool to the bone. Not much of a reaction to the revelation that the world's premier rappers knew his shit by heart. Eazy always played it real close to the vest.

I had been in the business long enough to know that when your act starts to glow white hot, your next move is to book them a tour. You do this for a couple of reasons. The main one, of course, is to capitalize on success—connect to the audience and pump the energy up even higher. Via radio interviews, ads on stations, and general street buzz, a tour becomes a self-perpetuating publicity machine.

But I also knew that when you remove an act from its home turf, you eliminate a lot of distractions. When you go out on tour, you go into the bubble. I wanted N.W.A. in the bubble right at that moment. If they had stayed in Compton as their record broke big, they would have been torn apart by their fans, like the Dionysian Greeks used to tear apart their gods.

To kick off the first national N.W.A. tour, I booked the band in Nashville just after Memorial Day in 1989, headlining a bill with Salt-N-Pepa, Kid 'N Play, Too Short, and Kwamé. A few dates on the tour would be coheadlined by LL Cool J. Atron Gregory, who managed an emerging rapper named Tupac Shakur, hired on as tour manager, with Gary Ballen as production manager. (That meant Gary handled anything related to production, while Atron handled all the rest.) Gary was the son of my father's sister, my first cousin, friend, and confidant, and a ten-year veteran of tour work. I wanted to have a capable guy inside who would report straight to me if things started to go south. The sound tech on the tour was a rapper named, confusingly enough, L.A. Dre.

One of my bedrock principles of agenting is that I never fly to a concert date if I have to take two planes to get there. If I couldn't fly direct, I wasn't going. It was a hard-won principle developed over the weary slog of the 1960s, waiting in too many chickenshit airports for too many white-knuckle commuter flights.

I could, of course, fly directly to that debut tour date, so I showed up at Nashville International to find Gary and Atron freaking out.

"They aren't here," Gary said, an edge of hysteria in his voice. All the Ruthless artists were supposed to have flown out from Los Angeles the day before.

"What the fuck happened?" I screamed. Back in those days, my drinking and high-blood-pressure days, I was a screamer with the best of them.

In the gaps between my screaming fits, the story came out. The Ruthless crew of twenty-nine people boarded a Southwest Airlines flight at LAX the previous day. Soon after the flight took off, however, there was a verbal dust-up with the flight attendant. Soon everybody had entered the fray. The flight made an unscheduled stop at Phoenix's Sky Harbor Airport, and the whole Ruthless entourage was escorted off the plane.

An auspicious beginning. I realized that you could take the kids out of Compton, but you couldn't take Compton out of the kids. I also knew that if they had been a boisterous white debating society, say, there probably wouldn't have been a problem.

We bought another round of airline tickets for the whole twenty-nine-person crew. The band made the concert on time. This was a "Platinum card" tour, with everything, including hotels, meals, and airline tickets for twenty-nine people, put on Jerry "Sugar Daddy" Heller's American Express Platinum card. My credit report was starting to glow in the dark.

I should have instructed them to leave Cube behind in Phoenix, where he could have continued his mechanical drafting career. He had hustled back into the group when the Priority deal was finalized, but he was always a major pain the ass—a complainer, a borderline paranoiac.

"A paranoiac," growled writer William S. Burroughs, "is someone who is in complete possession of the facts."

Well, Cube didn't have all the facts. He only thought he did. People ask me all the time what Cube was like to work with, given his outbursts on his later records, which surely rank up there as egregiously bigoted sentiments (check out his songs "Black Korea" or "No Vaseline").

But I knew O'Shea Jackson well. I knew his parents, Hosea

and Doris, both of whom worked at UCLA. Doris especially was very proactive on her son's behalf. I used to field calls from her all the time. She was a superintelligent, very capable woman. No son of Doris Jackson could possibly be a bigot. I don't think Cube was really anti-Semitic. I think he was pro–Ice Cube. He cynically but effectively used the prejudices of his community to gain purchase for his career.

Cube made one brilliant move on the N.W.A. tour. He did all the press he could. No one else from Ruthless was at all interested in talking to reporters. Interviewing Eazy would have been like interviewing the Sphinx. But Cube's public profile rose higher and higher that summer, keeping pace, almost, with his ego.

What the other band members were interested in doing, of course, was fucking any and all pieces of strange that came their way. Eazy hated male groupies. He simply couldn't stomach his legions of adolescent male fans. But he always had time for the troupes of females who flocked backstage.

He delighted in rubbing my face in it, too. On a concert date, Eazy telephoned my hotel room.

"Whyn't you come over?" he said. "I got some business to talk about."

I walked across the hall to his suite. The door was open. "We're in here," Eazy called from the bathroom in the bedroom.

I entered to find Dre and Eazy cavorting with a gorgeous naked girl.

"I want you to check those royalty statements Bryan Turner sent over for *Eazy-Duz-It*," Eazy said, totally bland. "Man, something don't seem right with the percentages on the mechanicals."

Eazy sat on the toilet with his pants down around his ankles.

Raisins. His first thought was to dump the whole thing in my lap.

My initial reaction was similar to Turner's. I recall my mouth becoming more and more parched as I read through the paragraphs of the letter for the first time.

Okay, so you don't believe that. You think, rather, that I was overjoyed at the pure unadulterated publicity value of it all. You wonder if I immediately sent Milt Ahlerich a check, memo'd "for promotional services rendered."

But you have to remember that I am a Jew, and for a Jew to receive a letter from the FBI brought up all sorts of terrifying history of knocks on the door from the Nazi gestapo, the East German Stasi, the Russian NKVD.

So fear was my first reaction, quickly followed by a crowing jubilation at the surreal, insane, totally unlikely absurdity of it all. Of course, I knew the letter would be pure gold for N.W.A. What better imprimatur could a rap group have than hate mail from the FBI?

To me, though, it was just one more expression of Newton's Third Law. Police pushed Eazy, Dre, and Cube every day of their lives. As members of N.W.A., they pushed back with "Fuck tha Police." Now the police community was pushing back at N.W.A.

I know many police and law enforcement officials to be honest, dedicated men and women. I would never advocate anyone taking pot shots at them. But in this country, protected as we are by First Amendment guarantees of the Constitution, they have no legal right to muck around in questions of free expression.

I wonder if the FBI ever sent a letter of censure to James Cagney when he glorified gangsters in *White Heat*, or to Johnny Cash when he sang his immortal line in Folsom Prison, glorifying cold-blooded murder: "I shot a man in Reno just to watch him die."

Milt the FBI guy also got his facts wrong. There were actually eighty police officers shot and killed in 1988. The next year, the year that the bloodthirsty gang from Ruthless Records went on national tour, stirring up antipolice hatred, that number went down to sixty-nine—still too many, to be sure, but contradicting the view that N.W.A.'s depictions of violence might actually foster violence.

Phyllis Pollack, the publicity director for Ruthless Records, went into overdrive mobilizing a response to the FBI initiative. Eventually we discovered that the letter was something of a rogue action by Milt Ahlerich. Even though he professed to articulate the "FBI's position" and the opinion of "the entire law enforcement community," he was essentially just a single pissed-off bureaucrat with a bully pulpit.

It wasn't Ahlerich's finest moment as a Fibbie. His off-the-reservation attack on N.W.A. earned him a transfer to the Bureau's backwater Hartford office. Oddly enough, he went on to become the security director for the N.F.L., overseeing the safety of professional football players who, of course, were always great fans of N.W.A.

I kept waiting for the other polished-black FBI shoe to drop. I removed sensitive documents from the Ruthless offices in case of an FBI raid. I didn't really think the government was going to suspend the First Amendment and haul my ass off to jail. But Ahlerich succeeded in stirring up the passions of police officers all across America, including those cops who Ruthless was paying to provide security for N.W.A. shows.

The mood turned ugly out on tour. In Cincinnati, N.W.A. was busted for violating the city's obscenity statutes, taking its place in a long line of artists, from actress Mae West to photographer Robert Mapplethorpe, victimized by the censorship capital of America.

Then, in mid-October, the light finally broke through. U.S. Congressman Don Edwards, a thirty-year member of the California delegation to the House of Representatives, chairman of the House Subcommittee on Civil and Constitutional Rights, and a former FBI agent himself, wrote a letter to FBI Director William Sessions that blasted the Bureau for its unconstitutional campaign against N.W.A. Wrote Congressman Edwards:

The FBI has developed an official "position" on a rap song by the group N.W.A. and has conveyed that position to the group's record publisher, Priority Records. I am afraid this smacks of intimidation. Officials of the FBI should not be music or art critics . . .

I do not believe that it is appropriate for the FBI to single out a particular song or film or book and write to its distributor. The only credible purpose of such an exercise is to encourage the distributor to drop its promotion of the work or the performer, and that would seem to be censorship.

As soon as I read Don Edwards's letter, I knew we would be okay. When you have a determined civil libertarian such as Edwards in your corner, it is unlikely that the goons in the FBI would pursue their vendetta against you.

Police move against Eazy. Eazy moves against police. FBI moves against Eazy. Congress moves against FBI.

Checkmate. Or so I thought. Years later, in 1994, the FBI confiscated a skinhead hit-list letter with Eazy's name on it. They alerted several other names on the list, but not Eazy. When our lawyer Harland Braun confronted the FBI about the lapse, the agents involved stated with a straight face that they didn't consider the threat against Eazy to be "credible."

Eazy-E: "Built like a tank but hard to hit"

threatening to quit. He said he wasn't being paid what he was worth.

"I write all the damn lyrics, don't I?" he wailed. I half expected him to break into a big Barry Manilow number. *"I write the songs that make the whole world sing."*

After a Columbus, Ohio, date, the other members of N.W.A. got together and talked about voting Cube off the island.

"He's gonna quit anyway," Eric said. "Let's toss him out before he does."

He came out of the meeting and confronted Cube. "If you want to leave, just go. Here's your ticket." He held out an airline ticket.

Cube was sullen, silent.

"You know who N.W.A. is, O'Shea?" Eazy asked him. "Me, Dre, Yella, and Jerry Heller, that's who. That's the core. Fuck yourself."

Even though Cube wasn't voted out of the group until the end of the tour, I knew what Eric and the others were really thinking. With Cube included, there were five members of N.W.A. The pie was split five ways. Without Cube, everyone got a bigger slice of the pie. According to Cube, of course, he quit the world's top-selling rap group at the top of its game.

"Trey can rap for us," Eazy said, meaning Tracy Curry, the D.O.C.

I didn't see how that would work. The D.O.C.'s throat had yet to heal from his accident. His voice was a whisper of its former self.

N.W.A., the group that Eric had hired me to protect and serve, was breaking up in front of my eyes.

Me and the "E" in Hawaii

Big Ron got on the line. "I don't do domestic problems," he said.

"What? What the hell are you good for?"

But Big Ron was probably right. More cops get killed on domestic disturbance calls than all other incident types combined. So I phoned Eazy on one of his multiple cells. "I'm going to kill the bitch," were the words with which he answered. "She totaled out the Beemer, Jerry!"

"Okay, listen," I said, the voice of reason. "Here's what I want you to do. Get out of that house. Just leave. Have Ron drive you to your place in Westlake."

Eazy had bought himself another house closer to the Ruthless offices in the very upscale Conejo Valley community of Westlake Village.

"What about my car?" he screamed. He was more upset than I had ever heard him to be.

"Go to Westlake. Listen to me. When you get there, there's going to be a brand-new BMW parked in the driveway. Fuck the 750, man. This one's going to be an 850ci."

"An 850?" Quieter now. Sulky.

"The only question is, what color do you want it in?"

"How you gonna get an eight-fifty delivered, middle of the night?"

"You let me worry about that. Just get in the car with Big Ron and get the fuck away from there before the police come."

Silence. I could hear Devil Woman snuffling in the background.

"Come on, man. I promise, the car will be parked in your driveway at Westlake Village."

He told me he'd go with Big Ron and hung up. Gary took

D.W. to Valley Presbyterian, blood streaming down her face.

I called Jeff Kagan, the dealer we worked with at Bob Smith BMW in Canoga Park. It was now a little after three a.m., but I had his home and cell number. I woke him up.

"Listen, you know that white 850ci we looked at last week? I need you to deliver that to a place in Westlake."

I gave him Eric's Westlake address. "The only thing is, you have to do it now. Otherwise no deal. Has to be parked in the driveway in an hour, by four a.m."

Kagen then said the only two words that any self-respecting car salesman could have said when tantalized with an order for a ninety-two-thousand-dollar luxury coupe.

"No problem," he said, and hung up. Ah, capitalism. Nothing's ever closed. Don't you just love it?

I considered the hefty price tag for Eazy's new car cheap when compared to a domestic disturbance beef, which would have impacted on Eazy's legal problems in all sorts of negative ways. One of my primary occupations at Ruthless was sorting out Eric's Byzantine family court affairs. We had a separate checking account just to pay his child support obligations, which ran to forty thousand dollars a month.

I've seen people mount up on their high horses over gangsta rap and its portrayal of women, and I always want to tell them to walk a mile in Eazy's shoes, or Dre's shoes, or even Devil Woman's shoes. D.W. never pressed charges. She continued to go out with Eric. She was a Compton girl, and eminently familiar with the terms of the contract, because she, like Eazy, had lived it all her life. I'm not saying it's right—I'm just saying it's *Wright*. It was Eazy's world, and I was just a guest in it.

"It ain't misogyny," Eazy said. "It's ghetto reality."

All of which leads to one of the most disgraceful episodes in the Ruthless saga, certainly a shameful aspect of Dre's story. In November 1990, Fox's *Pump It Up* ran a segment on N.W.A. and Ice Cube, both camps trading insults. The next month, Dre saw *Pump It Up* VJ Dee Barnes at a record release party and went medieval on her ass, slamming her face into a stairwell wall. When Barnes fled into a bathroom, Dre followed her in and pummeled her some more.

I knew Dre to be generally nonviolent and mild-mannered, but he was drinking that night. He used yet another UNLV football program bodyguard, Charles Wiley, to hold back the crowd as he beat down Dee Barnes.

"Yeah," MC Ren later said to a reporter, "the bitch had it coming." What made the incident more despicable was the fact that Dee Barnes was a longtime friend of both Dre and Eazy. And I was left to clean up the mess, fielding Barnes's twenty-two-million-dollar civil suit against Ruthless Records, in which I was personally named. The suit was settled out of court, and eventually Dre and Dee Barnes became friendly again. "I was in the wrong," Dre told the music press.

Dee Barnes with Body and Soul bandmate Rose Hutchinson

I haven't seen Cube since he left N.W.A., which didn't mean he was finished with dissing me in his songs. Years after "No Vaseline," he was a guest on a radio show with former-KDAY disc jockey Julio G. During an off-mike moment, Julio asked Cube why he didn't stop beating the dead horse of Jerry Heller.

Cube grinned sheepishly. "I've been doing it so long," he said, "that I can't stop now, can I?"

Well, technically, yes, Cube, you could—that is, if you were a man. But you're still locked in a "kill the authority" dynamic that you can only dimly understand, and certainly don't have the stones to confront in yourself.

There were a lot of people involved in turning Cube against Ruthless. Chief among them were Bryan Turner and his director of publicity at Priority, Pat Charbonnet. Turner had all his eggs in the Ruthless basket. We were by far the biggest moneymaker on Turner's label, and I think he wanted more control. Charbonnet was an enormously capable woman, an excellent publicist, but for some reason she and Bryan conceived the goal of making O'Shea Jackson a solo artist on Priority.

How could a fragile young ego such as O'Shea's resist Turner and Charbonnet's pitch? I can just imagine them purring to Cube: "You are the greatest rapper of all time. We can make you a huge star as a solo artist."

Of course, Eazy and I had the same goal, and we were further along in the planning of it. We scheduled the "Untitled Ice Cube Solo Project" as our next big release after the 1989 tour.

"We're putting a lot of trust in you, man," I told Ice Cube. "Don't fuck it up."

Which he proceeded to do. With poison being poured into

his ear and smoke being blown up his ass at the same time, the poor guy didn't know if he was coming or going. It turned out he was going—out of N.W.A. and off of Ruthless. His first solo release, *AmeriKKKa's Most Wanted*, came out on Priority, and Pat Charbonnet signed on as Cube's new manager.

Byran Turner got his way. Ice Cube was a huge success on Priority. But Turner accomplished his goal at the expense of breaking up the black Beatles. Turner shot himself in the foot. We could have put out two, three, four, a dozen more N.W.A. records, huge sellers that would have grossed hundreds of millions. Instead, Turner only saw the short-term goal of signing O'Shea Jackson—at least, that's how it looked to me.

But O'Shea's leave-taking was a "good riddance" development. For a brief moment in the summer of 1990, everything seemed to click. I managed the hippest, toughest band in the world. Ice Cube, the eternal troublemaker, departed to fuck with someone else's life. Dre, Eazy, Ren, and Yella went back in the studio, and put together the *100 Miles and Runnin'* EP to follow up the hugely selling *Straight Outta Compton*.

Eazy based the *100 Miles and Runnin'* title track on another of his all-time favorite movies, 1979's *The Warriors*. The great master of ballistic cinema, director Walter Hill, ranks in my mind with Sam Peckinpah for his depictions of America's favorite national pastime, which is violence. *The Warriors* tells the story of a gang accused of killing a crime lord, with all the other gangs in New York gunning for them. They have to get to their home turf of Coney Island, threading through a maze of violence worthy of a video game.

Eazy played the VHS version of *The Warriors* constantly,

almost as much as *King of New York*. It was odd, that for a Los Angeles guy, he was so enamored of New York movies.

Runnin' with my brothers, headed for the home base
With a steady pace on the face that just we raced

N.W.A. might have been missing Cube's lyric bite, but Dre's production raised the songs on *100 Miles* to the level of genius. From the sublime to silly: The EP's second track was "Just Don't Bite It," one of Eazy's sexual comedies that turned out to be one of his most popular cuts.

The EP took off like a shot. Everything N.W.A. did turned to gold. To commemorate the release, MTV hosted one of its infamous "pool parties" at Eazy's house in Westlake Village.

All through the early 1980s, in one of the most blatant cases of corporate-supported racism I had ever seen, MTV refused to put rap videos in heavy rotation. The boycott lasted for the first eight years of the music channel's existence. Viacom, MTV's corporate parent, never explained the policy. The channel simply ignored the largely African-American artists who played hip-hop. And MTV didn't just neglect to play our *Straight Outta Compton* music video. The channel officially banned it.

But the program *Yo! MTV Raps*, which debuted in September 1988, changed all that. We invited the show's celebrity DJ, Fab 5 Freddy, to host the pool party in June 1990. With "100 Miles and Runnin'" booming from banks of Westlake-rattling speakers, the party drew what looked to be half the twentysomething female population of Los Angeles County, bikini tops optional. Fab 5 Freddy seemed almost delirious, cackling and shouting like a madman. And director Ted Demme (Jonathan's nephew, who died in 2002 of an accidental cocaine-induced heart attack) caught it all on camera.

As usual, the police had a slightly different perspective from Ruthless Records'. Before Eazy and Dre moved in, Westlake Village was a sedate, predominantly white, and very upscale Conejo Valley enclave. In radio transmissions, the Ventura County Sheriff's officers routinely referred to Dre's compound as "the coon's nest." When Eazy took up residence, he was greeted with the words "Nigger Go Home!" spray-painted across his garage. Eazy shrugged it off.

"That guy don't know taggin'," he said, criticizing the bigot's graffiti style.

As the pool party cranked up to mini-Woodstock levels, police blocked off street access to Dre's compound. One of the guests of the party was a fifteen-year-old named Warren G, who came around with some Long Beach rappers calling themselves Nate Dogg and Snoop Doggy Dogg. In an upstairs bathroom, Dre and Eazy once again invited me to another sex-threesome business meeting, just like on tour.

Feeling as though discretion was the better part of valor, I went home early.

That might have been the high-water mark of N.W.A., the sex-drenched, music-fueled "MTV Wet and Wild Pool Party" under the Buick-blue skies of Westlake Village.

I saw some of Demme's footage of Eazy and MC Ren, laughing and mugging for the camera. It struck me once again how young all the Ruthless guys were. The boys of summer.

Me and Lorenzo
Rolling in a Benz-o

But that night, I did.

Suge, Dre, the D.O.C., and Michel'le went out and sat in Suge's vehicle. They left at around ten p.m. They were gone one hour, two hours, three hours. Normally, I didn't stay around the studio that late, but I wanted to see how this would all play out.

"They outside talking," Big Wes answered when I asked him what was going on. He didn't volunteer more information.

What could they be talking about all that time? I wondered. I looked over at Eazy: oblivious.

After that night, Dre began to go missing. He skipped studio dates. When I did see him, it was in passing. It wasn't quality time. All he would do is complain constantly about not getting paid, not having money, not getting what was due to him.

Suge barged into the office of Ira Selsky, Ruthless's lawyer. He announced to Selsky that he needed Dre's employment contracts, and he wasn't going to leave until he got them.

Selsky felt physically threatened. He ran out of his office to call me. I told him that Suge could have copies of the contracts, since Dre, the D.O.C., and Michel'le had all instructed me to give them to him.

Left alone, Suge rifled through filing cabinets and took the whole folder containing Dre's Ruthless contracts. It was a ridiculous move, since of course we maintained the originals at Ruthless. But it served its purpose, increasing the atmosphere of menace that had begun to hang around Ruthless in the fall of 1990.

We received a visit from Suge and his crew at the Ruthless offices, too. As I sat at my desk in the same chair Suge had so nakedly coveted, I suddenly found myself invaded. Suge Knight and three of his man-mountain homies swept in all at once. My hand strayed under my desk, where I kept a .380 handgun affixed to a peg.

"Don't bother," said one of Suge's goons. He made a pistol of his thumb and forefinger, like a little boy playing cops and robbers, and brought it up to my temple before I could move. "I wanted to, I woulda had you."

He clicked his thumb and said, "Bang!" very softly.

"Your bodyguards ain't shit, Jerry," Suge said. "You better get some new ones."

Then he was gone.

I decided to take Suge Knight's advice. Ruthless needed reinforcements. Across the parking lot from the first Ruthless offices near Lanark Park, an Israeli named Mike Klein ran a dance wear manufacturing company. We became friendly, and I gradually understood that Klein had a background in the Israeli security forces. He didn't talk about his past, but he carried himself like a man ultimately confident in his ability to handle any situation that came his way.

We stayed in touch even after Ruthless moved its offices to Woodland Hills. After the Selsky incident, I called up Mike Klein.

"We've got a situation here," I told him, "and I thought maybe you could help us with it." I explained what was going on. By the end of that conversation, I agreed to hire Mike Klein as the new security director of Ruthless Records. (Later on, Eazy made him director of business affairs.)

The effect was immediate and extreme. Somehow, the Suge Knight camp had Klein checked out and realized they were now dealing with a Mossad-type motherfucker who didn't fool around. Suge vanished. His crew vanished. An uneasy calm descended.

But the beef didn't end. The strategies merely changed a bit. Instead of direct confrontation, I began to get late-night phone calls, heavy breathing hang-ups. Eazy reported being occasionally tailed on his nocturnal forays through South Central.

We were at war. And right in the middle of it, I fell in love.

Gayle Steiner appeared regularly as an actress on *Baywatch*, but after her incredible face and figure got your attention, she followed up with a finely honed sense of humor and a quick intelligence. It was a one-two punch that I found irresistible. While I hesitated to bring anyone into the shit storm my life had become, I realized at the same time that I desperately needed someone.

Gayle helped immensely to stabilize my ups and downs, calm my anxieties, and generally relieve the almost unbearable tension I was experiencing because of Ruthless. The night I met her, we talked about music. I asked who she listened to.

"I guess I'm mostly a metal fan," she said. "Metallica, you know, Guns N' Roses."

I started naming bands that I had once managed. "You like Creedence? Van Morrison? Otis Redding?"

"Sure," she said. "Classic rock." I suddenly realized how young she was. She hadn't been born when those artists hit their peaks.

She asked me what I did. "I manage the black Beatles," I said.

Beyond being a *Baywatch* babe, Gayle turned out to have an unusual history. Both her parents had died when she was still a teenager, and she helped take care of her younger sister, Vicki. Gayle did everything she could to keep her and her sister afloat.

*October 19, 1996, the best day of my life: the beautiful Gayle Steiner,
aka Mrs. Jerry Heller, and me*

everything I could to forestall the breakup of N.W.A. Because of the new computerized SoundScan sales-tracking system, the Billboard album charts were much more accurate and much less open to corrupt industry massaging. *Efil4zaggin* shattered all the myths about the limited market appeal of hip-hop when it debuted on the charts at number two. A week later it bumped Paula Abdul's *Spellbound* out of number one, taking over the top spot.

Efil4zaggin, which is "Niggaz4Life" spelled backward, was, from strictly a production point of view, even more interesting and innovative than *Straight Outta Compton*. Julio G, the KDAY DJ, called it a better album than *Compton*. Not everyone agreed, since *Efile4zaggin* clearly showed the impact of Cube's departure. Sonically, it was superior to everything that had come before. Verbally, it was not.

The tracks pushed Eazy's outrageous sexual humor further than ever before, on parodies such as "She Swallowed It," "Automobile," and the fake-soulful "I'd Rather Fuck You." Some of the cuts were broad skits, while others were more ominous, including a mini drama Eazy called "To Kill a Hooker." The second cut was the masterpiece, a droning, minor-key epic called "Real Niggaz Don't Die."

All in all, *Efile4zaggin* was an album to throw gasoline on the flames. Parents hated it. Fans embraced it to the tune of three million in sales—another platinum record for Eazy's walls at Ruthless.

I was a rationalist. Why in the world would anyone in their right mind break up a number-one band with a hit record? It just didn't make sense.

In November 1991, Dre came to Eazy and me crying poverty. "I don't even have money for Christmas this year," Dre said.

Eazy scowled. He had no pity, no "ruth," like the etymology says.

I thought we should extend an olive branch to Dre, maybe kick-start negotiations for him to remain at Ruthless.

I gave him a check for forty thousand dollars.

"You're such a damn sucker, Jerry," Eazy said as soon as Dre had left. And he was right. The payment bought us no good will at all.

Working desperately to salvage Ruthless's relationship with Andre Young, I brokered a twenty-million-dollar deal with my old protégé Irving Azoff at Warner. The deal would have allowed an immediate payment to Dr. Dre of two million dollars. It would have kept N.W.A. together and ensured the vitality of the Ruthless brand.

Mo Ostin vetoed the deal. Milt Ahlerich, the author of the FBI letter, had won after all. Ostin was clearly spooked by the incredible anti-hip-hop backlash that rolled over the country then, inflamed by the FBI letter, by the controversy about Ice-T's song "Cop Killer" and N.W.A.'s "Fuck tha Police." These modern-day James Cagneys weren't going to be allowed to create their gangster personas, not if the literal-minded fascists who ran this country had anything to say about it.

I had run out of options. My last-ditch hail-Mary effort failed because Warner Brothers lacked the courage to back an artist in the face of public controversy.

Reluctantly, Eazy and I went to a sit-down at a law office with all the principals involved. Suge Knight was there with Dre, who hid behind dark glasses and said not a word during the whole hour-long conference. Suge's white lawyer, a greasy-haired, ponytailed scumbag named David Kenner, sat on the other side of him. Virgil Roberts, Dick Griffey's right-hand man, stood up and said he was there as "a friend of the court," but I told him since we weren't in court I didn't know what that meant so he should sit down and shut the fuck up.

On Dre's behalf appeared a lawyer named Angela Wallace, dressed to the nines in a black miniskirt, as foxy as a legal representative could possibly be. She has since been imprisoned for financial irregularities, and is no longer a member of the California bar.

On our side of the table, for Ruthless, were Eazy, myself, and security director Mike Klein, plus our lawyers Bob Dudnik and Ira Selsky.

I went through the motions, but I was sick at heart. David Kenner kept repeating that we should not worry, that it would all work out. It never did.

I couldn't see the conference as anything but a funeral wake for N.W.A., the world's most popular band at that time. And yet, here we all were, gathered around a butcher's table, ready to cut the throat of the goose that laid the golden egg. The same thought kept going through my mind: *Why can't these guys work this out?*

There's such a long tradition of music acts not letting acrimony get in the way of business. Sam & Dave, the original blues brothers, hated each other with a passion. They never spoke. They'd show up for a concert, go onstage, do their act, and leave without exchanging one word. They had a long and productive career. If Sam & Dave could do it, so could N.W.A.

Which brings to mind the famous exchange between Roxie and Velma in Bob Fosse's *Chicago*, when the girls were considering going into show business:

Roxie: It'll never work.
Velma: Why not?
Roxie: Because I hate you.
Velma: There's only one business in the world where
that's no problem at all.

I was a business guy, and what I was seeing around the conference table that day was bad business.

"Bidness is bidness," is how the D.O.C. used to say it. One of my bedrock principles in the music business was never to make artistic decisions based on financial considerations.

So we take a year, two years, even three years off. Could you imagine how huge an N.W.A. reunion album and tour would be?

But it was not to be. The golden goose was executed, plucked, carved up, and sold to the highest bidder.

Eazy stared across at Dre for the whole duration of the sitdown. Dre shifted in his seat uncomfortably. For once, he wore sunglasses and Eazy left his eyes uncovered. As the negotiations ended, Eazy spoke up softly during a gap in the conversation.

"Did you know about this, Andre?" He didn't have to explain what he meant by "this." Dre knew Eazy was talking about the Incident.

Did you know? Did you really set me up and deliver me into the hands of my enemies?

And I guess I was wrong about Dre not saying one word through the whole conference. Because he responded with a single word to Eazy's question: "No."

Whether he meant "No, I didn't set you up" or "No, I won't answer you," Eazy had no way of knowing.

N.W.A. is dead. Long live N.W.A.

Elton John and me in my backyard. "Jerry," he once told me, "you're the only man I've ever met in my life who can't keep time on a tambourine."

EXPRESS YOURSELF

The best of times were always just before you got here

I

In 1963, the world poised on the brink. Over the course of the next few years everything would change. Kennedy had beat back the Russian missiles in Cuba but wouldn't be around to answer the British Invasion of the Beatles and the Stones. The year itself belonged more to the sedate, conventional fifties than to the swinging sixties.

I got out of the army and drove my little MG convertible back to Los Angeles. I worked in a bank. I took night classes in business at USC graduate school. But I was restless, unhappy. That "something's coming" vibe featured in *West Side Story*, the most popular musical of the day, infected me like a virus. The voice of Shondor Birns ("Go in and take, kid!") replayed in my mind.

Not many people can say this, but my life was changed by a Las Vegas lounge act. My cousin Bill was in a singing group called the King's IV. He played the Frontier for seventeen years straight, alongside acts such as the Mary Kaye Trio ("You Can't Be True, Dear"), the Treniers ("(Uh Oh) Get Out of the Car"),

"No, I got it," he said the first night we all had dinner together. I reached for the bill anyway.

"Let the Commander get it," Philadelphia Jack said to me.

"Why?" I asked, ready to chip in my share.

The Commander reached into his pocket and brought out what looked to be a compact money roll held together by rubber bands. When I looked more closely, though, I saw it was a fat stack of a couple of dozen credit cards, along with driver's licenses from almost every state.

This was the age before computers. If the bill was less than one hundred dollars, the restaurant didn't have to call in the charge.

I am ashamed to say I was at least indirectly complicit in all this. I introduced the Commander to all my restaurant contacts, including the former owners of Martoni's.

"I'm going to be here every night," the Commander announced to them. "I'm going to pay for everything. Sometimes, if the bill is four hundred dollars, I'm going to ask you to run it through ninety dollars at a time." The Commander lowered his voice conspiratorially. "Some day, the FBI is going to show up and ask you about me. Is that a problem for you?"

Back then Martoni's was a mob hangout. Nothing the Commander said sounded even remotely like a problem.

"Okay, Paul," the Commander said to me after Martoni's gave us the green light.

"My name's Jerry," I reminded him.

"No, you're Paul," he said, handing me a credit card. "You're Paul Kaufmann."

I looked down, and sure enough, that was the name on the

card. A road forked for me right there, and I could have gone either way. But I handed back the card.

"No thanks," I said.

The last night before he was going to leave town for the winter, the Commander got busted at Disneyland for smoking. Back then, Disneyland was an authoritarian state worthy of George Orwell. Walt's stormtroopers wouldn't even let you in the place if you had long hair. The Anaheim cops tried to pull the Commander from his car in the Disneyland parking lot, but he led them on a merry chase all the way to the Vine Street freeway off-ramp in Hollywood.

He called me from jail. "You've got to get me out of here before they run me through the Federal system," he said. The Commander had a criminal record that would set off fire alarms he was so hot, but it would take the cops a little while to link the man to his crimes. Every minute inside brought him closer to a reckoning.

I called a bail bondsman I knew named Joey Durando. Dealing with musicians, you get to understand the true worth of the bail bondsman, a tragically under-appreciated figure in our society.

Joey Durando sprang the Commander, and the Commander swore himself forever grateful to yours truly. He decided to throw a farewell party for himself upstairs in a private room at Martoni's. The bill came to $2,500, a healthy check back in the mid-1960s. The Commander peeled a credit card off his roll and the Martoni's owners dutifully ran it through multiple times.

Sure enough, a month after the Commander blew town, a couple of guys in suits and FBI shoes showed up at Martoni's.

"We need to know about this customer of yours, Paul Kaufman," the FBI agent asked.

Tony of Martoni's shrugged. "He's just a customer."

"Wait a second," the agent said, getting stern. "This guy came here every night for three months. He threw a party and you ran his credit card through thirty times. And you don't remember him?"

"This is a very busy restaurant," Tony told the FBI. "We get a lot of people here. I don't remember everybody."

The first deal I ever made at Coast was for the jazz singer Mister B., Billy Eckstine. Marty Klein turned the booking over to me, to negotiate with a guy named Tats Nagashima, who was the biggest promoter in Japan in a couple of ways, since he stood six three and towered over most of his countrymen. Tats would do the Dylan concert memorialized on the album *Bob Dylan at Budokan*.

I booked Billy Eckstine for thirty-five thousand dollars. It was my first deal, and I was proud of myself. As soon as I brought the paperwork to Milt Deutsch, though, he started screaming at me.

"You stupid asshole," he yelled. "Look at this! Five thousand is firm and the rest is in options!" Nagashima had taken advantage of my inexperience. We eventually became lifelong friends, and I came to cherish this first, lightning-quick lesson in the harsh realities of show business.

Another lesson came when I got a call from a Sacramento club owner named Ned Hakim. Hakim made me a healthy offer to book Mickey Rooney in his brand-new club, the Cleopatra.

"Rooney is Milt Deutsch's guy," Marty Klein said, "so you have to go up there and scout the club, make sure everything is kosher."

I flew to Sacramento, and Hakim's Cleopatra Club was indeed fabulous, a huge confection of Egyptian-themed architecture. One problem: It was a strip club.

Deutsch remains at the top of the list of the nastiest guys that I've ever met in my life. He called me Feet 'cause I had big feet.

"Feet, I hear you got a booking for the Little Guy," he said when I called him to report in. That's how he referred to the diminutive Mickey Rooney, at the time at a low ebb in his career—"between comebacks," as we used to say.

"The club is spectacular," I reported back. "It looks like Caesar's Palace. But it's a strip club."

"For twenty-five grand, Mick would play a kid's birthday party," Deutsch said. He flew up to join me with his star client. I picked up Marty Klein and we drove together to the Cleopatra. As we approached the club, I got a sick feeling in the pit of stomach when I saw the marquee. THE CLEOPATRA PRESENTS CLARITA, it read.

Below, in smaller letters, were the words, AND M. ROONEY.

Klein and I had to get a ladder and physically change the billing.

At one time Deutsch had been a legendary agent. I kept hearing stories of the glory days. But he just got burned out on alcohol and ass-kissing, until he was a spiteful, malicious husk of a man.

We had to drive him everywhere to prevent DUI murders. He went to lunch every day at either the Friar's Club, where he met his running buddy, *Bonanza*'s Lorne Greene, or at Scandia, the superb restaurant across Sunset Strip from the Roxy, with the best food in town. Regulars there were called Vikings, with their own bucket-size highball glasses monogrammed with their names.

Deutsch had his routine. He'd go to the bar first, the bar-tender would pour a twelve-fingered drink for him, he'd take a big gulp—and spew it all over the nearest customer, pretending to cough. What a guy. He thought it was hilarious.

I was carting him to Scandia one day in my brand-new Cadillac convertible. As we parked on Sunset, Deutsch leaned over and hawked a big luger onto the floor mat in front of him. I couldn't believe it. I got out, walked around the car, and yanked him from the passenger seat by his silk fucking necktie.

"Feet, Feet, I was just kidding," he laughed. But I left him on the curb and drove away to look for a car wash that would clean up sputum.

I told Philadelphia Jack that working for Deutsch was driving me crazy. "I stay at Coast, one of us in going to die."

Philadelphia Jack just laughed. "You shouldn't take him so seriously," he said. "Milt's just a mean drunk."

I told him I had to get out.

"There's this guy named Bobby Phillips over at ABC, Associated Booking Company. They're sort of getting into this rock and roll stuff that you're interested in."

I said I would love to talk to someone at ABC—anything to get me out from under Milt Deutsch.

"It's a mob company," Philadelphia Jack said. "Owned by Joe Glaser, you know—Louis Armstrong's guy—and Sidney Korshak."

Sidney Korshak. The Fixer. The underworld's power broker. Not many people knew who Sidney Korshak was, but I did.

I shrugged my shoulders. I had come up with Shondor Birns. I wasn't going to be bothered working under Sidney Korshak.

I always got along well with mob guys. I used to tell them all the same thing. "I had a tough time making it in the army," I'd say. "I couldn't picture going to the brig for even a day. I'm not what you people call a stand-up guy, okay? If there's something that you're going to talk about that you don't want anybody else to know, ask me to leave the room."

I said, "I don't mind, I won't get insulted, I won't be embarrassed, because the first time a cop comes to me and says, 'Either you're going to jail or that guy is,' I will say, 'That guy's going!'"

And the mob guys would always laugh at me. But every time after that, whenever anybody began to talk about something they didn't want me to hear, they told me to get the fuck out of there.

"This guy, Phillips, I know him well," Philadelphia Jack continued. "I'll call Bobby for you and you can go over there and have a meeting with him. There's only one thing: He's going to quiz you. You've got to memorize the Billboard Top One Hundred. Bobby Phillips is going to ask you, like, 'What's number forty-six?'"

It was nothing to me. I had just gotten out of college. Memorizing the Top 100 just meant a little cramming. The Associated Booking offices were on Rodeo Drive at Brighton Way, where the Chanel boutique is now located, but back then there was an anonymous-looking three-story office building with Pagano's hair salon on the ground floor.

(The salon's owner was a stylist named Al Pagano. His nephew Jon Pagano Peters became Barbra Streisand's hairdresser and was used as the model for the character in Warren Beatty's movie *Shampoo*. Peters wound up running Columbia with Peter Guber, and getting hired to helm Sony Pictures.

From cutting hair to cutting movies: thus was the path to power in Hollywood.)

I first walked through the doors at Associated in July 1966, the summer before the Summer of Love. Bobby Phillips had thick, rose-tinted glasses. "There's one rule when you're in this office, kid," he said to me. He told me that in his locked, lower right-hand desk drawer, there was a phone. "When that phone rings, it's going to be Joe Glaser or Sidney Korshak. You get the fuck out of the office while I talk to them. Got that?"

I told him that I got it.

"Okay, you start at one seventy-five a week."

"Just like that?" I said. "You're hiring me?" I couldn't believe it. I was making $125 at Coast.

"Philadelphia Jack O'Brian says you are into rock and roll, so that's good enough for me."

"Aren't you going to quiz me on Billboard's Top One Hundred?"

"What?"

"Philadelphia Jack said you were going to throw questions at me, ask me what number forty-six was."

Phillips started to laugh, and I realized that I had been had. "You be sure to tell Philadelphia Jack I said hello," Phillips said, still laughing.

As I left his office, Phillips called me back. "Hey, kid, what is number forty-six?"

"Ruby and the Romantics," I said, lamely but automatically. "'Our Day Will Come.'"

He started laughing again as I headed down the hall out of the building.

Me with the first group I ever signed, The Standells, who, despite their frilly appearance, were responsible for the proto-punk hit "Dirty Water"

II

RESTAURANTS I HAVE KNOWN AND LOVED: PART TWO

There has never been a place and there will never be a place again like the Luau in Beverly Hills. I could see the restaurant from my second-story office at Associated Booking. There was an Arco gas station across the street and right next to it was the Luau. I'd park my car at the Atco station after work and head over to the restaurant.

You entered the Luau to another world. The tiki craze had probably crested by then, but someone had forgotten to tell the owners. The main dining room boasted several waterfalls. The drinks came with little brightly colored paper umbrellas in them. The place was owned by Steve Crane, Lana Turner's ex-husband, and Al Mathis, who drove a white Rolls Royce that he always parked squarely in front of the restaurant.

The Luau was the place. Everybody went there. At the door stood Joe Stellini, the host. His nickname was the Maltese Falcon because he had such a perfect profile. He was six three, one of the best-looking guys I ever saw, and he became one of my best friends. He was twenty-four years old but had a safe deposit box stuffed with cash, because everyone tipped him with tens and twenties.

At the Luau I began my habit of having dinner at the bar. To this day I prefer to eat at the bar of a restaurant because that's where the action and the energy always are.

Every young future movie star in the world was at the Luau. Jack Nicholson and the Roger Corman crowd hung out. Doug McClure and the pretty-boy Hollywood elite. Steve McQueen and his motorcycle pals. There was always a scattering of sixteen-year-old high-school girls from Beverly Hills whose fathers were the wealthiest guys in the world. And mobsters. David Fried and his father Happy Meltzer had a table next to the big waterfall, where they would sit every night with Johnny Roselli and Johnny Stompanato.

I had a booth. Aaron Spelling had a booth. Booths at the Luau were like wombs. They gave birth to careers. I never seemed to meet a person who was over twenty-five. Everybody shared the same drug dealers. It was a time when LSD and cocaine and pot were part of the social scene. Bikers were in the social mix too. Dennis Hopper hung out at a restaurant-bar in Beverly Glen called the Café Four Oaks, and he and his Harley guys would ride down to the Luau en masse.

But there was never a fight at the Luau. No one was looking to shoot anybody. Nobody was looking to beat each other up. It was peace and love all around. Everybody was trying to make a name for themselves. And where do you go to make a name for yourself? To Hollywood. There's sunshine. Beautiful women. Show business. For a brief shining moment in the mid-1960s, the Luau was Hollywood.

The Strip, on the other hand, was rock 'n' roll. From the Luau, a right on Santa Monica Boulevard and a left on Doheny Drive brought us to that section of Sunset Boulevard immortalized in the TV show *77 Sunset Strip*. The stretch of Sunset between Crescent Heights and Doheny was fast becoming as important to rock music as Memphis or Liverpool. Clubs, restaurants, and hangouts studded the Strip like diamonds in the rough: the Whisky A Go-Go, the Galaxy, the Trip, the Roxy, and Sneaky Pete's.

Just off the Strip, at Doheny and Santa Monica, Doug

Weston's Troubadour became a hotbed for new acts. Next door was Dan Tana's, another of my favorite watering holes.

The Strip had always been an entertainment mecca. There were a couple of reasons for this. By a quirk of city boundaries, that section of Sunset Boulevard long remained unincorporated territory, controlled by the much more lax Los Angeles County Sheriff's Department, rather than the hard-on LAPD. A loophole in the county tax code took a smaller bite of agency commissions, which resulted in a lot of agents flocking to the Strip, further contributing to its aura of lax morals.

By the mid-1960s, though, the guard was changing. Old-line clubs like the Trocadero, the Mocambo, Romanoff's, and La Rue had closed down as their clientele died out. The ultimate marker of the old Strip giving way to the new Strip came when the Byrds played their famous dates at the old-line Ciro's in 1965, kicking off the California rock revolution. A young publicity guy named Bobby Gibson headed the Group, representing acts like the Byrds, the Stones, the Doors, and the Mamas & Papas, at the same time running a nightclub called the Cheetah on Santa Monica Pier.

The Strip was where rock royalty hung out, and I was a young prince of the Strip because I hung out with them. The summer of 1966 turned into a continual rolling party, shaggy-haired, hazy-aired, and intense. The Strip was a place where people actually did "fight for their right to party," as the Beastie Boys would later put it. The Sunset Strip Riots that summer were a series of pitched battles between young rock fans and police intent on enforcing curfew.

My running-and-funning buddy of that time was Jack Kellman, a wealthy Chicago kid, heir to an auto-glass fortune, who wanted to get his kicks before settling down to the family business. We cemented our relationship—and our status as Sunset Strip desperadoes—one evening when we were late to an assignation with two young lovelies at my house in Benedict Canyon, and found ourselves with a busted transmission.

"If we wait for the tow truck, the girls are going to be gone," I said to Kellman. "They're not going to wait just because we had car trouble."

The car, a 280SE 3.5 Benz convertible, wouldn't budge in forward gears, but worked fine in reverse. To the cheers, catcalls, and applause of the late-night rock fans crowded on the Sunset Boulevard sidewalks, we drove backward all the way down the Strip from the Rainbow at Doheny, pulled a right in reverse, which was really confusing but was probably really a left, up Benedict Canyon Drive to 1627, where I lived. And our dates were still waiting when we pulled up ass-backward to my house.

If the Strip was the Emerald City of the Land of Oz, then Topanga Canyon was the haunted forest, full of flying monkeys and other sixties hippy oddities. All the Los Angeles canyons were stocked with musicians, artists, and hangers-on, but Topanga was the absolute outer orbit. There were people there who lived in refrigerator boxes.

Some of them I think I represented. Canned Heat ruled Topanga with a benevolent hand, as Bob "the Bear" Hite crawled out of hibernation every once in a while to play a squalling, scorching set of the blues at the Corral Bar. The Heat were the perfect jam band, because Hite's partner, Allan Wilson, would wail on endless harp and guitar solos.

Canned Heat was a powerful band in another sense, because they had Skip Taylor as their manager, the best drug dealer in town. Taylor once made a holiday delivery to my house of a healthy-size vial of Peruvian marching powder. "Have a White Christmas," read Skip's note.

Practice all the blues licks you want. Assemble a vast record collection, the way Hite and Wilson did. They were both virtual musicologists. But what made the Heat a true power in the business was not the licks, not the album collections, but the fact that their manager had the best drugs on earth.

All the animals came out of the hills to hear the Heat at the Corral. Janis Joplin was a regular, swigging her trademark Southern Comfort. I would like to boast that Janis sat on my lap numerous times during those nights, but it wouldn't be that much of a claim to fame. She sat on everybody's lap.

I was a *pisher*, but on the Strip, in Topanga and at the Luau, I thought I was an important guy. I didn't realize right away that there were two main reasons why people came over and said hello to me at the Luau, two reasons why people returned my calls. Those two reasons were my bosses at Associated Booking, Joe Glaser and Sidney Korshak.

I worked at Associated for months before I was aware of Sidney Korshak's presence. That was always Korshak's MO. He was the figurative man behind the curtain. He controlled the Riviera and the Dunes casinos in Las Vegas. He represented the hotel workers union in Las Vegas, the Teamster's Union Pension Funds, and IATSE, which was the powerful stage hands union in Hollywood. Sidney Korshak was a man who could shut the town down. He was best friends with MCA chairman Lew Wasserman, and the two of them ruled Hollywood like a medieval duchy—Wasserman as the industry's more-or-less public face, Korshak as the shadowy fixer.

If Korshak was known at all, it was for his trademark eighteen-karat-gold Dunhill lighters. He bought them by the caseload. Whenever he lit a woman's cigarette, he would gift her with the Dunhill he had used. There were hundreds, maybe thousands of Korshak's elegant gold lighters in women's purses all over Hollywood.

It turned out that, for me, Korshak was also very literally the man behind the curtain. I never really noticed it, but there was a gold drape hanging next to the switchboard at Associated as you exited the elevator on the second floor. I must have walked by it a thousand times on my way to my office before I ever went through it.

One day I was sitting at my desk when I got a call from Bobby Phillips. "The Man wants to see you," Phillips said, and hung up.

I was a *pisher*, but I wasn't dumb. I knew who the Man was. The summons to Sidney Korshak's office should have struck fear in my heart, but it didn't. I was saddled with that lethal one-two combination of youth: arrogance and ignorance.

Okay, I said to myself, *I'll just go up and see the Man.* But I had a problem. I didn't know where the Man's office was.

"I need to see Mister Korshak," I said to the switchboard operator. "Where do I go?"

She motioned with her head toward the gold curtain. I fought my way through the heavily-woven folds of velvet drapery and found myself facing the door to a private elevator. I got in the elevator and saw there weren't any buttons to push. The doors merely closed and the elevator whisked me upward to a kind of bomb shelter on the roof. I know that's a strange sort of oxymoron, a bomb shelter on a roof, but that's exactly how Sidney Korshak's office struck me.

The elevator spilled me out into an elegantly appointed space with an aircraft-carrier-size desk. Behind the desk sat the six-foot-four éminence grise of Hollywood, gray-haired and handsome. Like a lot of mob guys of his generation, Sidney Korshak had adopted the practice of keeping a jar of candy on his desk, only his was about four feet tall, filled with jelly beans. His partner Joe Glaser was more of a caramel corn kind of guy.

I introduced myself to Korshak, took some jelly beans when he offered them, and sat down.

"Some friends of mine are going to come over to your office," he said.

And that was that. The phrase "friends of mine," when it came out of Sidney Korshak's mouth, meant something very specific.

The friends of Sidney Korshak's who visited my office a few days later were three guys and a singer. The three guys were all dressed the same way, in the "Continental" look: black kid-mohair suits, immaculate white shirts, and thin silver ties—*Reservoir Dogs* when Quentin Tarantino was still in diapers.

The young singer had evidently sucked all the style from the other guys. He was dressed to the nines. He wore thick rose-colored glasses à la Bobby Phillips.

Reservoir Dog number one sat uncomfortably close to me at my desk. There were no introductions at all.

"We want him to play twelve weeks at the Riviera and twelve weeks at the Dunes." These were the first words out of the mouth of Reservoir Dog number one.

"Well, okay . . . ," I said, trying to hide the fact that I was dubious.

"Do you want to hear him sing?" Reservoir Dog number one asked me. "Kid, sing for the guy."

"He doesn't need to sing," I said. "I know his record."

They wanted thirty-five thousand dollars for the first four weeks, forty thousand for the next eight weeks at each casino, a primo deal that amounted to several hundred thousand dollars. I told them I'd have to check with Mr. Korshak. Reservoir Dog number one reacted with a look of impatience.

"So call," he said.

"Just find out how they want the contracts made out, and how they want it split up, and where they want it to go to," Korshak told me on the phone.

I issued the contracts on the spot, while the singer and the Reservoir Dogs were still in my office. As far as I know, the singer never played Vegas, nor received any of the money. The checks went to whomever they were supposed to go to.

Welcome to the music business, Sidney Korshak style.

My work at Associated wasn't all no-show contracts and smoke and mirrors. Most of my clients were passed on to me via the higher-ups, but I made my own way in the world too.

It didn't take a genius to recognize genius in the music world. All you had to do was ask yourself a series of questions.

Who was the most successful girl group ever? The Supremes. What was their label? Motown. Who was the most successful male R&B group? The Temptations. What was their label? Motown. Who was the most successful child prodigy? Stevie Wonder. What was his label? Motown. Who was the most successful family group? The Jackson Five. What was their label? Motown.

What single music executive created the label that harbored every one of these acts? Berry Gordy Jr. He also assembled the greatest stable of songwriters ever, including Holland-Dozier-Holland and Ashford and Simpson.

Out of respect for his accomplishment, I always addressed the chairman of Motown as Mr. Gordy. He was the man. You don't discover and develop that many superstar acts by accident. I was in awe of Berry Gordy. As an agent, my responsibility was to go where the talent was, and a huge pool of talent collected under Motown's umbrella.

Motown was a womb-to-the-tomb kind of operation, with its I.T.M.I. talent-management wing teaching the House of Hits artists how to walk, how to dress, how to act on stage. Mr. Gordy was a consummate businessman, scrupulously honest within the context of the music business, which means something quite different from the context of most businesses. It doesn't mean he was dishonest, but he wasn't in it for charity, either. In other words, Berry Gordy was not above using tactics like his famous paper bag filled with cash in order to get a leg up.

The paper bag strategy was very simple, and it had variations with Cadillacs or other prizes as the lure instead of the paper bag. When signing an artist to Motown, Gordy would often slide a whole shitload of money in a paper bag across his desk. Now, if the artist or his representative took the money, he probably was signing away publishing rights to all his songs in perpetuity. It was a lousy deal for the artist, but the dazzle of up-front cash was just too much for some people.

Gordy had the integrity not to punish an act that was smart enough to refuse the paper bag. But he lived in the real world enough to attempt the strategy. Just business.

Another aspect of Gordy's genius was that he assembled executives around him who were among the best in the business. A consummate operator named Shelly Berger was responsible for the Supremes. I worked with a Motown executive named Larry "Max" Maxwell. Max was one of the guys who believed in me before I believed in myself.

I was a mere child, green as grass in the music business, but for some reason Max took a liking to me. I became Larry Maxwell's go-to white man. He produced and managed all of Motown's second-tier groups: the Four Tops, who were one rung below the Temps; Martha and Vandellas, who were a notch under the Supremes; and Marvin Gaye, whose first three Motown singles had been unsuccessful, and who had not yet broken out to superstar status. Of course, "second-tier" is relative, and at any other label these would all be top-tier acts.

Eric Burdon of the Animals used to refer to Gaye as "St. Marvin of the Brokenhearted," but to me he was always the black Sinatra. He was that talented. After I became Marvin's agent, we were joined at the hip throughout his Tammi Terrell period, when the two singers had hits doing Ashford-Simpson-penned duets such as "Ain't No Mountain High Enough," "Your Precious Love," and "You're All I Need to Get By."

"I'm going to drop out of show business," he announced to me one day. "I want to try out for the Detroit Lions."

Far be it from Pete Southern's grandson to stand in the way of anyone's sports career. I wished him luck. He was serious. He bulked up to 210 from his normal weight of 150 pounds. He had excellent speed. Marvin was the last guy cut in the Lions' training camp that season. We were back in business.

But business with Marvin Gaye never ran entirely smoothly. He was a playa before there was such a thing as a playa, into gambling, golf, drugs. He was mercurial and hard to contain. It was with Marvin Gaye that I first cemented my reputation as an agent who could work with difficult acts.

It wasn't always easy. When Marvin was rehearsing to go on a TV variety show hosted by the roly-poly comic Jonathan Winters, he saw me standing backstage. He stopped midsong and crossed over to me.

"I want those glasses," he said.

I was wearing three-hundred-dollar French Tropicale sunglasses with blue lenses that I had just purchased at a highline boutique. I told him I would be happy to buy him his own pair the next time I visited the store, but that he couldn't have mine.

"I'm not going out unless you give me them." He raised his voice. "I'm not doing the show," he said to the producers.

By that time I was sick of Marvin's whims and divalike behavior. I refused to give up my blue Tropicales. And he refused to do the show. Later he adopted blue-lensed sunglasses as his trademark.

My intransigence didn't sit too well with my bosses at Associated. But I was unrepentant. I always maintained a certain level of mutual respect with the acts I represented. I would go to the wall for my artists in contract talks. But I refused to become anyone's butt-boy.

The black Frank Sinatra, my star client, "St. Marvin of the Brokenhearted"

III

Everyone who lived through the sixties was transformed by them. The decade was part full-immersion baptism and part shock to the system. It was the best of times, it was the worst of times. The Summer of Love, the summer of the Haight, the Days of Rage. The sixties broke open the human spirit and let a little sunshine in. But the decade also killed Janis, Jimi, and Jim Morrison, and gave us Charlie Manson, Charles Whitman, and Richard Speck.

Tim Leary said if you remember the sixties, you weren't there. I was there, and I remember.

The dark side of the sixties came into my life one afternoon at my house in Benedict Canyon, courtesy of a friend of mine named Gary Stromberg. Stromberg had a bad habit of bringing strange people into my life. He introduced me to Philip Kaufman, who kept a solemn oath to his friend Gram Parsons by stealing his buddy's body from the undertaker, transporting it to Joshua Tree, and immolating it in the desert. Stromberg also set me up with another "friend" who crashed at my guest house and set up a meth lab there without my knowledge.

So I should have been forewarned the afternoon Stromberg called me on the phone. "I've got a guy," he raved. "He's got these tapes and he has all these chicks with him and they're hot and we need to come over to your house."

Anyone in their right mind would have said no, but for a whole decade in the middle of the last century, no one in America was in their right mind.

Soon enough a ragtag group of hippie women invaded my house like poison gas.

In those days I had a great place on a fabulous piece of

property in Benedict Canyon. It was a beautiful spot. The tenant before me was Terry Melcher, Doris Day's son and a big record producer who worked with the Beach Boys.

The hippie girls settled in as though they owned the place, sprawling over a big bed that lay on the floor of the master bedroom. At their head was a ragged-haired ex-con, who sat cross-legged on the bed and played a tape of himself tunelessly beating out songs on a guitar. The girls hung on his every word. I recognized Charlie Manson instantly for what he was: a pimp-trained hustler. I had seen many more like him bottom-feeding on the Strip.

I stood it as long as I could. This was, after all, the sixties, the dawning of the Age of Aquarius. Hippies were people too. But finally the whole scene started to bore me. I turned to my buddy Jack Kellman, who towered over the scrawny Manson and outweighed him, too.

"Tell that scumbag he has to leave," I told Jack.

Charlie didn't argue. The girls sullenly got to their feet. By kicking them out, I had violated the peace-and-love spirit of the age. Charlie gave me the stink eye as he filed past me with his deodorant-challenged harem.

It turned out that Manson had been to the house before. I didn't know it at the time, but Charlie had a beef with my predecessor in the house, Terry Melcher. Manson thought Melcher had reneged on a promised record deal. He was a pig in Charlie's eyes, suitable for slaughter.

A few months after our brief encounter, Charlie sent his minions back to Benedict Canyon. On the night of August 9, 1969, the Manson girls and their cohorts showed up at my front door, confused, gunning for Manson's archenemy, Melcher.

Luck, or karma, sent me elsewhere that evening, shepherding Lee Michaels through a gig at the Fillmore West. So the Manson crew instead invaded a house right around the corner from mine, at 10050 Cielo Drive. For a lot of people, the sixties ended right there, with the murders of Sharon Tate and her four houseguests.

Later, when the reality of my close call had sunk in, I called up Gary Stromberg. "A meth chef, a body burner, and now Charlie Manson," I said, referencing the trifecta of the world's greatest lunatics he'd sent my way. "Listen, man, do me a favor and please don't introduce me to any more of your friends."

I represented another sixties icon in the person of Emmett Grogan, the founder of the Diggers in San Francisco, whose personality was an odd combination of ethereal and scary. The Diggers were the quintessential sixties phenomenon, a Haight-Ashbury collective that advocated abolishing money. Free love, free dope, free food.

Grogan ruled over the Diggers by sheer charisma. He and his minions would commandeer trucks (people would thoughtfully leave the ignition keys in them for the Diggers' use), go to restaurants and get their leftover food, then take it to Golden Gate Park and feed the homeless every day at three o'clock.

Emmett Grogan became a friend of mine through Alfie Schweitzman, who used to work for Bob Dylan's manager Albert Grossman and was the road manager for Delaney, Bonnie & Friends. Schweitzman came to work for me and introduced me to Grogan, a legitimate tough guy who for a time was Bob Dylan's bodyguard.

The first time I met him, we were all together at a house I rented in Franklin Canyon: me, Schweitzman, Jack Kellman, Grogan, and

Rick Danko and Richard Manuel from the Band. Danko and Manuel had a studio back then in Malibu, at Broad Beach. I called the Liquor Locker and had them deliver a case of Jack Daniels and a half dozen cases of beer. Schweitzman had a dilapidated Mustang, a wreck of a car he had just driven out from the East Coast. He parked it across the street from my house.

By eleven o'clock we were all as drunk as human beings can possibly be, and I got a visit from my across-the-street neighbor. He came to the front door of my house, which was a Dutch door with the top half open.

"Listen, can you move that fucking piece-of-shit car that is parked in front of my house?"

In back of me, I felt Grogan, Kellman, and the others stir in the darkness of the living room. I almost started laughing. This neighbor of mine didn't know who he was fucking with.

"I'll tell you what," I said. "I'll park my Rolls in front of your house for a week. How would that be? Then you can tell everyone who saw the Mustang that the Rolls is yours."

The surly neighbor abused the hospitality of my Dutch door a little longer, and then left. But the more I drank, the drunker I got, the more the incident infuriated me. I reached under my couch for a chrome-plated .32 that I kept there.

"Where are you going?" Kellman asked as I rumbled toward the door.

"That motherfucker across the street," I slurred. "Fuck him." My brain had taken a vow of silence, but the Jack Daniels was talking big.

Grogan decided he wasn't going to let me leave the house drunk and carrying a pistol. The five of them—Grogan, Kellman, Schweitzman, Danko, and Manuel—managed to take me down. They proceeded to dismantle a baby grand I had in my living room, ripping out piano wire and using it to tie me up. Grogan sat on my chest until I calmed the fuck down.

When Grogan left the next day, he gave me a copy of his great autobiography, one of the forgotten masterpieces of the 1960s, *Ringolevio*. In honor of the Battle of the Dutch Door, he inscribed the book: "To Jerry Heller, a stand-up guy (at least the first time around, motherfucker)." He told me that I was going to be his agent, and would make the movie deal for his book. Grogan became my buddy for life.

After that I began spending more time in San Francisco, the center of the sixties maelstrom. Every couple of nights I'd drive down to Big Sur to the Nepenthe coffee house, perched dramatically on a cliff two hundred feet above the angry surf. Johnny Rivers, Joan Baez, her sister Mimi Fariña, and other Big Sur artists would congregate at the Nepenthe, sitting around a bonfire with guitars, trading songs.

"Oh, man, you should have been here last night—Bob Dylan played the Nepenthe song circle!" I must have heard that a half dozen times. The poet of the generation always seemed to have been at Nepenthe just the night before, never the night I came. It always reminded me of that line about New York: "The best times in New York City were always just before you got here."

The journey from the touchy-feely Nepenthe song circle to the gritty music world of San Francisco should have been measured in light years. Back then I booked Ike and Tina Turner, and Ike got ensnared in a San Francisco date that introduced me to the muscular politics of the Black Panthers.

"I got this date," Ike informed me. "But I don't have to commission you on it, motherfucker, because I booked it myself."

"Yeah?" I said, accustomed to Ike's surliness. "Who are the promoters?"

"Bobby Seale, Rap Brown, and Huey Newton," Ike said.

"You're playing a concert for the Black Panthers? You understand who these people are? They walked into a police station in Oakland one Sunday and killed a bunch of cops. They're at fucking war with the police."

"Yeah, yeah," Ike said, raising a black power salute. "Right on." He thought he was being funny.

"These are the most serious and committed people around," I said. "They aren't going to pay you, Ike. They are going to expect you to donate your payment to the Party."

"Fuck them, man," Ike Turner said. "I'm tougher than them."

Well, Ike *was* pretty tough. I just didn't know if he was as tough as the Panthers. He carried a Thompson .50. He was infamous for having beaten Tina. He was, by the way, one of the great guitar players of rock 'n' roll. George Harrison called "River Deep, Mountain High," the gorgeous love anthem produced by Phil Spector and featuring Tina Turner's powerful vocals, "a perfect record—from start to finish there's not a single wrong note."

All that was well and good, but I had had run-ins with the Panthers before. I went to a sit-down with Emmett Grogan and some Panther operatives in the Prospect Park area of Brooklyn. Every single member of the party had a shotgun on his lap. The scene recalled Bogart's line in *The Big Sleep*: "My, my, such a lot of guns around town and so few brains."

I was as pistol-happy as the next guy, but the Panthers gave off a strong-arm aura that I didn't want to get involved with.

"I'm telling you right now, Ike," I said. "I am not going to have anything to do with this date. I am not issuing any contracts on it. I'm not talking to them, I'm not doing anything with them."

True to my word, I didn't go to the concert. The Panthers gave Ike his fifteen-thousand-dollar payment in cash. Ike put the money in his dressing room with a couple of bodyguards to watch over it. While he was onstage, he had a straight sight line to his dressing room door from in front of the mike.

Ike looked backstage and saw that the Panthers had his bodyguards at gunpoint. They busted into his dressing room and retrieved their money.

"Those fucking Panthers!" Ike shouted into the mike. "They're taking my money! This fucking concert is over."

The Panthers rushed onstage and beat Ike Turner with lead pipes. They put him in the hospital for two weeks.

When he got out, he came up to my office. "I got a problem," Ike said. "The Panthers want to have a meeting with me."

"So have a meeting with them," I said. "You're the fucking tough guy, Ike. This is all on you."

Somehow, Ike talked me into taking the meeting with the Panthers. The negotiations for the sit-down went on for several days, as though we were trying to set up a presidential debate. What city? Who brings what bodyguards? Who gets naked first in the strip-down search for weapons and wires?

The Panthers finally agreed to meet at my office. Huey Newton was there. With him was a woman who carried the most enormous carpetbag-style purse that I had ever seen. *I wonder what she's got in there,* I remember thinking. Also in the group was the Iceman, the "Minister of Defense" for the local Panther chapter.

"Take your clothes off," the Iceman said to me.

"You think I'm taking my clothes off in front of you guys?" I said. "I got a little fucking tiny dick, and I'm sure as hell not getting naked." I had a three-piece suit on, so I took my jacket and pants off. The woman with the carpetbag left the room.

"Ike's got to make good on his concert," Huey said.

"I can't let him do that," I said. "You didn't pay him, and instead you beat the shit out of him and put him in the hospital."

"How about we kick your ass instead?" the Iceman said.

"You can't really threaten me, because unless you are ready to do it right now, there's really nothing you can do to me."

I knew what the meeting was. It was a negotiation. No one screamed or yelled. If you didn't hear what was being said, you would almost describe the mood as cordial. We decided that Ike Turner would withdraw his accusations of assault against the Panthers. But he wouldn't have to play a makeup concert for the group, either. Huey and the Iceman got up and left my office, taking the woman with the big carpetbag along with them.

After that, whenever I went to San Francisco, I didn't wear a flower in my hair. I wore a gun in my belt.

John was the guy with whom to negotiate. He was a former stockboy at San Francisco's Fantasy Records, which had signed the band as the Golliwogs, with Tom as the lead. Fantasy released single after single from the Golliwogs, songs such as "Don't Tell Me No Lies" and "Little Girl," none of which burned up the airwaves. Then producer Saul Zaentz bought Fantasy Records. The band changed its name to Creedence Clearwater Revival and put John up front as the lead singer. The rest was rock and roll history.

"You know something?" I said to John. "You don't need me. You don't need anybody. You are going to be one of the biggest stars in the world. But I can make your life a whole lot easier."

Though we never signed a formal contract, I was Creedence's agent from that point on until I left Associated. The Fogerty brothers, Stu Cook, and Doug Clifford, the band members of Creedence, were all tough East Bay guys. As we were on a plane flying to a date in Phoenix, some drunken rednecks started to make fun of John's hairstyle. As was his wont, John sat alone, away from the other band members. This was the late sixties, when long hair should no longer have been an issue. But nobody had told these rednecks that.

"Look at the girly with the long hair," one of them shouted. "Hey, girly, you want to come sit on my lap?"

Fogerty said not a word in reply. The rednecks kept heckling him, calling out, "Where are you going, girly-girl?"

Fogerty suffered in silence. The rednecks finally stopped for a while, but started up again just as we landed in Phoenix.

"Hey, girly—come on home with us!"

Suddenly Fogarty got up, and Tom, Stu, and Doug joined him, looming over the hecklers.

"We'll meet you out there on the tarmac," John said. "Then we can sort out who the girls are around here."

Creedence deplaned and waited, as promised, on the runway. And the heckling rednecks refused to get off the plane. They would not leave. John and the boys had put the fear of God into them.

For handling Marvin Gaye, the Rascals, and for bringing Creedence into the agency, Associated Booking gave me a raise to $225 a week. In today's terms, that sounds like a pittance, but I had extremely low overhead. I was single. I was paying my rent, I was driving a Cadillac, I was going out every night. I had a great apartment just below the Sunset Strip clubs. No matter how drunk I got at the Whisky, I could always just roll home. It was downhill.

Even with this lifestyle, I was spending no money at all. Somebody—Capitol, Columbia, Warner—always had a record release party going on. Some of the guys were at William Morris, some were at ICM, some at ABC, but we all had expense accounts. We were all good-looking, well-dressed guys, and the publicists from all these companies were good-looking young women. The music business back then was an incredibly incestuous scene. Someone was always picking up the tab.

The levy was much lower then. For sixty dollars, I used to take a date out to dinner at Dan Tana's, say, or Sneaky Pete's. A steak, everything you could eat and drink: sixty dollars. It was great. Even at $225 a week, I was living high.

But I still had no contacts at all in the real heart of the music business, the record companies. I knew agents and mobsters and DJs. I had started to get to know promoters, the frontline shock troops of music, the guys who actually booked the halls and hired the acts. But on the other end of the business spec-trum were the record companies, and that world was still a mystery.

What changed the situation for me was a guy named Jerry Cohen, who came to me at Associated with a group that was signed to Dunhill Records. A burly, Joey Buttafucco–style guy who was five-feet-seven tall and almost the same across. Cohen's family owned all the vending machines in San Diego County.

"Listen, I got this group," Cohen said to me. "They used to call themselves the Thirteenth Floor, and I just changed their name to the Grass Roots. I want you to book them for me."

Slowly I learned about the quite maculate conception of the Grass Roots. A pair of producer-songwriters named P.F. Sloan and Steve Barri released a song called "Where Were You When I Needed You," credited to a band called the Grass Roots. But there was no actual band—the name was just a convenient tag for Barri and Sloan's projects. But when the song hit big, they needed a real band to tour. Enter Jerry Cohen and the 13th Floor.

Newly reconfigured as the Grass Roots, the band became enormously successful with straight-ahead California rock, an AM-radio version of the Byrds. Sloan and Barri's next song-writing creation, "Midnight Confessions," was a huge hit with Warren Entner on vocals and keyboards, Creed Bratton on lead guitar, Rob Grill on vocals and bass, and Rick Coonce on drums.

The group's label, Dunhill Records, was owned by Lou Adler (nowadays known to millions of basketball fans as "the guy in the hat" who always sits next to Jack Nicholson courtside at the

Lakers games) and a former tap dancer named Bobby Roberts. Roberts teamed up with John Phillips from the Mamas & Papas to mount the groundbreaking Monterey Pop Festival in 1967, still the best fucking music festival ever produced, Woodstock notwithstanding. Bobby Roberts brought in his brother-in-law to run Dunhill. His brother-in-law was named Jay Lasker, an insurance salesman who, unlikely as it was, turned out to be a record-promotion genius.

Boxing commentators always say Roy Jones was pound for pound the greatest fighter in the history of the fight game. Well, dollar for dollar, Jay Lasker was the greatest record man ever born. He was a little older than the young Turks coming up in the business, and he was funny-looking: wall-eyed, a little dumpy. But he was an ace.

The ABC television network bought Dunhill Records, and ABC made a little mistake with Jay Lasker. The network negotiated a salary based on records shipped. So, of course, Lasker shipped as many as he could. It didn't matter how many actually wound up in the hands of consumers. Hey, a deal is a deal.

Padded totals or not, geeky-looking insurance salesman or not, Lasker achieved legendary status in the industry, eventually landing as chairman of Motown.

I met him way back when, at Dunhill. Suddenly, through the Grass Roots, the record company world broke open to me like a ripe pumpkin. I was in.

Because of the way my father brought me up, I had comfortable relationships with Jewish guys who were older than me. I showed them respect. When I dealt with guys that were very smart, like the executives at ABC/Dunhill, I always took the same tack.

Don Biederman, who would go on to run Warner Chapel Music, and Ira Selsky, who would eventually became the lawyer for Ruthless Records, both represented ABC/Dunhill back then.

"Look, I haven't done this before," I said to the two of them and Lasker. "If you fuck me, you're just going to embarrass me with the act. Don't embarrass me. Give me a good contract. Be fair with me and I'll always be fair with you."

In the cutthroat music business, that type of honesty isn't supposed to work, but it did. I didn't know contracts that well as of yet. I always told the Jewish executives I was negotiating with to skip past the "goyim draft," the first onerous contract draft that heavily favored them.

Jay Lasker was my guy. The Grass Roots used to battle him over insane little record-release details. They were a big act. They sold records. And they would fight with Lasker as if he were the devil himself.

"What the fuck are you fighting about?" I asked Warren Entner.

"He wants to make this album cover purple!" Entner responded, as if it were self-evidently the most absurd idea in the world. Entner was a smart guy, the leader of the Grass Roots, and a man who became a dear friend. He wound up marrying a Miss Universe and went on to manage Rage Against the Machine and Quiet Riot.

"So what?" I told him. "It doesn't matter."

"But it's *ugly*."

"Yeah, so? It doesn't matter. You want to get Lasker mad at you so he doesn't promote your record? Just let him do what he wants. You're good at what you do. Let him be good at what he does."

I was born a Libra, and I knew that the good goes with the bad. I also knew that Jay Lasker could sell records. He might not have been able to design album covers, but he was one of the great ones.

So was Clive Davis at Columbia. When Davis invited me to form a joint venture with him at Columbia, I took it as a validation of everything I had been doing up to that point in time. In my eyes, Clive was the man at the pinnacle. He epitomized everything classy, intelligent, and successful about the record business. We called our label Great Western Gramophone, and released albums by the blues band Glencoe and the supergroup Sweet Thursday (with Beatles and Stones keyboardist Nicky Hopkins, guitarist John Marc, and the horn player Johnny Almond).

Jay Lasker. Clive Davis. Like Larry Maxwell at Motown, they believed in me before I believed in myself. I felt as though I was working with people at the top of their game. I was about to meet a few more.

Me and the boys: Terry Ellis (far left), who managed Jethro Tull, Ten Years After, and Robin Trower; and Don Tarleton (far right), one of Canada's biggest promoters

V

Bill Graham could go from zero to sixty faster than any man I've ever met, igniting into screaming fury at the drop of an option clause. He was perfectly capable of going to war over a case of Coca-Cola not specified in a contract rider as a backstage amenity. He used to signal he was mad at you by tearing up your Rolodex card into little pieces and mailing it back to you. In San Francisco, where he ran venues such as Fillmore Auditorium, Fillmore West, and Winterland, Bill Graham was the man. He wasn't limited to San Francisco, either. Graham was the first guy to do tours coast to coast, a one-man Clear Channel before that company ever existed.

He was also my guy. Since I was putting acts into his venues on a weekly basis, I spoke to Graham almost every day. It often wasn't pleasant. If I didn't take his call, he would scream at my secretary, behavior that I found unconscionable. He and I often wound up pushing the triple-digit decibel range shouting at each other over the phone. But I always recognized Bill Graham as the world's greatest rock impresario.

Bill used to hold up the fingers of his hand and tick the fingers off. "Artist, manager, agent, record company," he'd say, and then he would wag his thumb. "The promoter. The only one that interacts with all the others."

Just like Bill, to take credit for the evolutionary development of the opposable thumb. He always put himself at the center of the universe. Actually, I knew that the manager was the captain, the true opposable thumb.

But witness what Bill Graham accomplished. Over a one-month period at Fillmore West, a young music lover in San Francisco could have seen the following acts, courtesy of Bill

Graham: Santana, Chicago, Otis Redding, the Byrds, Joe Cocker, Eric Burdon, the Grateful Dead, the Who, Ike and Tina Turner, Iron Butterfly, the Doors, Canned Heat, Fleetwood Mac, Jethro Tull, Lee Michaels.

Every third name on that list represents an act that I booked. I may have had a love-hate relationship with Bill Graham, but I loved his concerts. The man knew how to treat an audience, and how to show off artists.

One month. And those were just the headliners. There has never been a time when so many major acts came together in so short a period at such a great, middle-size venue as the Fillmore. Graham learned show business at the Borscht Belt resorts of the Catskills in New York. As a kid he had walked across Europe to escape the Holocaust. Before Bill Graham, the rock scene was just a lot of stoned-out hippies noodling on guitars. No one could figure out a way to make money putting on rock 'n' roll shows until Bill Graham showed us how. He was manic, detail-oriented, relentless. He and I were a good fit.

In March 1969, I was at the Fillmore for a Creedence date. I watched from backstage as Ian Anderson of Jethro Tull led his band through a blistering set. The audience had never seen anything like it. Here was this raggedy haired flautist doing the standing-on-one-foot crane position from martial arts, with his bandmates generating a squall of English noise behind him. It was a transcendent experience.

Anderson came off the stage. Terry Ellis, his manager, stood there, an exquisite contrast to Anderson in his pink, button-down shirt. Anderson blew past Ellis and slammed his fist into a set of backstage lockers.

"What fucking shit!" he bellowed. He paced back and forth

like a caged animal, blowing off stage energy. I could tell Anderson really felt hangdog. He wasn't just falsely modest, fishing for compliments. He actually believed the astonishing forty-five minutes of music I had just listened to had somehow been less than stellar.

He refused to do an encore. The crowd was about to rip the Fillmore apart, demanding one.

Bill Graham and I cornered Anderson. "Say something to him," Bill said to me.

"Ian, man, you've got a whole different set of standards from the people out there. Your mediocre is their extraordinary, you dig?"

Yes, people really did talk that way back in the sixties. But Anderson calmed down. "Are you listening to them?" I asked "They didn't think it was shit! They thought it was fucking far out, man!"

"You made the audience happy, didn't you?" Bill Graham asked, repeating his favorite mantra. "Now go out and make them happy some more."

Ian Anderson nodded numbly and trudged out to bless the audience with another performance, "mediocre" by Ian's standards, extraordinary by anyone else's.

When I had the Average White Band appearing in San Francisco, I witnessed another side of Bill Graham: the angry god side. The venue had an alley in back of it, and I was standing at the mouth of the alley with Arif Mardin, Average White Band's producer, and the elegant and high-line Steve O'Rourke, Pink Floyd's manager. Floyd was also in town at the Cow Palace, and the three of us were enjoying the atmosphere, which may or may not have been suffused with San Francisco's excellent drug supply.

Bill Graham pulled down the alley in a magnificent brick-red Jaguar XKE series 3. I was seized with a cotton-mouthed case of auto-envy. The car resembled a huge shiny penis. Bill Graham's was bigger than mine. He had a look on his face as he drove slowly by us as though we were street urchins and he was the big cheese.

Then he pulled out onto Post Street and a cop car smashed into his car at high speed.

We had just witnessed an accident. It was sick, but before we even were certain that Graham was all right, we all broke up laughing. We couldn't help it. Bill leaped out of the Jag and stood there staring at it, paralyzed with rage. For a penniless child who trudged out of Europe during World War II, that car must have represented "I made it" as if the words branded across his forehead.

He glared at the cackling street-urchin fools in the alleyway, the peanut gallery for his catastrophe. There was nothing he could do. If an ordinary citizen had destroyed his car, Graham might have been able to give him a solid thrashing, but because it was the police, all he could do was stand there and boil. I know spontaneous combustion in humans is supposed to be a myth, but whoever said it was never saw Bill Graham in a rage.

I met him that night backstage at Winterland. We spoke. He didn't mention getting his car totaled that day, and I didn't either. We never talked about it. The wound was too raw. As soon as I got back to Los Angeles I priced Jaguar XKE's.

I always figured if I could handle the mercurial Bill Graham, I could handle anyone. I've had relationships with some of the most volatile figures in the music business. At the Troubadour one night, I stepped in the middle of a face-off between two of the five-hundred-pound gorillas on the scene back then, David Geffen and Albert Grossman.

Grossman was a music manager par excellence, the man who created a hit act with three folksingers named Peter, Paul, and Mary, the business muscle behind Bob Dylan, Paul Butterfield, Janis Joplin, Delaney Bonny and Friends, and the Band. Geffen at that time was just starting his meteoric rise through the ranks of the entertainment business. He had blown through William Morris and Ashley Famous talent agencies before forming his own management company with Eliot Roberts.

Monday at the Troub was Hoot Night, which always attracted an assembly of industry heavy hitters. The news on everyone's lips that night was David Geffen's amazing deal to sell Laura Nyro's publishing company, which David half owned, to Clive Davis at Columbia for three million dollars. None of the young Turks in the music business (and I was one of them) had ever dreamed of those kind of numbers. Geffen made the underground real.

Not without a few bumps along the way. It turned out that Albert Grossman felt that Geffen had reneged on a deal to sell the publishing rights to a friend of his.

Grossman confronted Geffen at the Troub that night. "Let's go out in the alley and talk," Albert said to David.

David was small, but so is a grenade. He was fearless. He walked outside with the big, bearlike Grossman.

Standing with Jeff Wald, Helen Reddy's husband and manager, and PR genius Bobby Gibson, I watched the diminutive Geffen leave braced with Grossman. It didn't seem fair to me.

"David's going to get his ass kicked," Gibson said.

"You really think we should let that happen?" I asked.

Gibson and I followed them outside. The Troub had an alley beside it off Santa Monica Boulevard, between the club and Dan Tana's restaurant. Grossman loomed over Geffen in the alley, screaming at him. *Next come the fists,* I thought. Grossman was a serious hard-ass. Sure enough, he backed Geffen against the wall of the Troub.

"Hey, hey, cool it out, man," I said as Gibson and I walked up. "What's going on here, Albert?"

Grossman blathered about Geffen promising Nyro's overseas publishing rights.

"You know, Albert," I said, "maybe you can get away with this type of shit in Woodstock or New York or London. Not in Los Angeles. This is my town. You don't come out here and start yelling at people. That's not going to fly. Yell at him when you catch him in New York, man. Not out here."

Grossman left. Geffen didn't thank me and Gibson for evening out the odds. I'm sure he thought he could have handled them. But after that I enjoyed a smooth, mutually beneficial relationship with Geffen, at least for the next couple of years.

He showed up at my thirtieth birthday party at my bungalow in Beverly Glen, along with every member of the Sunset Strip rock pantheon and the music business hierarchy. Actually, it was my thirty-first birthday, but my pals Bobby Gibson and *Midnight Special*'s Susan Richards threw me the party and decided it would be more impressive to call it my thirtieth. Gibson had a press agent's malleable approach to age. "All rock stars, no matter how old they are," he told me once, "are always nineteen."

The party was raucous. Beverly Glen was the Laurel Canyon of Beverly Hills; only Laurel was full of dope dealers and the

Glen was full of dope users. Geffen showed up, stayed briefly, and presented me with a staggeringly nice gift: a pair of diamond-and-gold Van Cleef and Arpels cuff links. I could see at a glance they were fabulously expensive, two or three grand at least. A tribute for my heroism at the Troubadour perhaps? I concluded that I was a better friend to David Geffen than I had thought.

Back then I didn't know a French cuff from a French maid. I was more of a Mahitibel shirt guy—the elegant, flowery, ribbony hippie garb turned out in her small shop at Vermont and Western, very popular in the rock world. Mahitibel used to sew small hidden pockets into my collars so I could take cocaine on a plane. Since I didn't wear French cuffs, I returned David's cufflinks to Van Cleef and Arpels to exchange them for some silver Corum wristwatches I liked. I got three of them in the trade, with faces of green, blue, and mother-of-pearl. But when the store manager put the transaction through, I found that David's cufflinks had originally been a gift to him, a present from Atlantic Records head Ahmet Ertegun. I had been re-gifted.

I laughed off the incident and enjoyed my watches. But my smooth relationship with David was about to end.

I had an office at 9121 Sunset, in a building that *American Bandstand* impresario Dick Clark owned. The rent for the office came with lunch on Fridays included, brought in by Dick Clark himself, who would always eat with us. He was the best. The nicest guy in the world.

At around this time, I got a very earnest handwritten letter from a University of Illinois student named Irving Azoff. Azoff badly wanted to work in the big-time music business. He had promoted several concerts while he was in college, and would be willing to move to Los Angeles or New York, his letter stated, as soon as he got a job offer.

I liked the kid's chutzpah. So I offered Irving Azoff a job as an agent. I didn't know at the time that Azoff had sent identical letters to an elite list of music people, including David Geffen, who was just starting Asylum Records, and Frank Barsalona, the hall-of-fame agent behind Premier Talent. But I was the one who hired him. Irving wouldn't stay long with me. He was intent on moving as quickly up the ladder as he could.

One act that Irving brought with him from Illinois was a young folksinger named Dan Fogelberg. While still at the University of Illinois, he sent Fogelberg's demo tape over to Clive Davis at Columbia. Besides being the most elegantly dressed executive in the business (it's a neck and neck race, or necktie and necktie, between Clive and Atlantic's Ahmet Ertegun), Davis had the best ears in the business for a song.

"He's not quite ready," was Clive's judgment on the Fogelberg tape. Irving and I thought he was, so we shopped that demo all over Hollywood. One person we gave it to was David Geffen. He pounced. He loved Fogelberg.

"David's not right for Fogelberg," I said. "He's got too many male vocalists on Asylum as it is, with Jackson Browne, David Blue, Ned Doheny, and Jo Jo Gunne."

I thought for a beat. "Send the tape to Clive."

Irving shook his head. "He already heard it and said Dan wasn't quite ready, remember?"

"Don't worry," I said. "Clive won't remember what he listened to three months ago."

I was right. Clive Davis declared the "new" Fogelberg material sensational, much better than the last (identical) batch. He signed the singer to Columbia's Epic label, along with Irving's other act, REO Speedwagon.

I then had to deal with David Geffen's ire. I was poised to do a lot of business with David. I had just done the Crosby-Nash acoustic tour, which was a fabulous success and garnered great reviews. Geffen was very persuasive. He had talked me into doing that tour for 5 percent, half my usual agent's commission, the only time in my professional career I had ever cut my commission. But Geffen promised me the next tours of both Neil Young and Joni Mitchell—at full commission.

With David, you were either his friend or his enemy. There was no middle ground. When I gave Dan Fogelberg to Clive Davis, I crossed over the line. Geffen immediately gave away the tours he promised me to Danny Weiner, another agent. He would no longer take my calls.

Geffen was easily the equal of Bill Graham in the screaming-mad-ballistic category. Like a lot of small guys, including Irving Azoff and Eazy-E, Geffen used the phone as a cudgel. The telephone is a great equalizer. No one can tell how tall you are when you are speaking via PacBell.

Besides, Geffen was a lot taller standing on his money. Hands down the most successful entertainment executive of the modern era, he didn't get to start record labels and movie studios by being a shrinking violet. And he proved it when I finally had Irving get him on the phone.

He didn't say hello, just launched right into the screaming. I screamed back at him for a little while, then I lost my patience.

"David, come to the window."

"What?"

"Come to the window." Our offices were both on the second

floor, facing each other across Sunset Boulevard, mine at 9121 Sunset, his at 9120.

Geffen came to the window across the street. "Hey, David," I called out to him. "Here's what I think of your taste in music."

I began tossing Neil Young and Joni Mitchell tour posters out the window. Their albums, their promotional materials, anything and everything remotely connected to the man staring gape-jawed at me from his office window. The material fluttered down amid the traffic on Sunset Boulevard.

"Next time I see you," I shouted, "I'm going to put you over my knee and spank you!"

I slammed shut the window. Azoff looked as though he thought I had lost my mind, which I had.

"Fuck it," I said. "I'm not doing anything with him anymore."

One of the albums hit the shoulder of Jerry Brandt, walking on the sidewalk below. Brandt was head of the rock and roll division at William Morris, and happened to be Geffen's former boss at the agency. After he got hit with a flying Joni Mitchell projectile, he immediately came up to the office.

"I just wanted to meet the guy who dealt with David Geffen that way," Brandt said.

It was a burned bridge to which I would dearly regret putting the match. Geffen, of course, rose higher and higher into the entertainment firmament. I was on permanent suspension in David Geffen's world.

Irving Azoff dodged that particular bullet, going on to work closely with Geffen, rising parallel with him to manage the Eagles, Jimmy Buffet, and Christina Aguilera (among others), to become chairman of MCA Music, to found Giant Records, and to grow into a legendary figure in the music business. For me, it was a road not taken, a road, in fact, that I had impulsively strewn with land mines. I didn't have a choice. The artist came first.

I pretended that I didn't care. I fashioned myself after independent guys such as Frank Barsalona, the agent behind New York's Premier Talent, the world's first and finest agency devoted exclusively to rock acts. Barsalona was at once my main role model and primary competitor. I also admired one-man, one-act managers such as Floyd's Steve O'Rourke, Led Zeppelin's Peter Grant, the Guess Who's Don Hunter. I studied agents such as Howard Rose, who repped Elton John after I did his first tour and had the best mind for the mechanics of a deal of anyone who I ever met.

Associated was a very powerful agency, but by the end of the 1960s I was getting restless there. I felt overworked and underappreciated. I had made friends playing liar's poker with an ex-William Morris agent named Don Fischel, a mild-mannered Casper Milquetoast who you didn't always want to ask how he was doing, to avoid getting an earful of woe. Fischel was a rock-solid agent, and he knew I was unhappy at Associated after I complained about getting stiffed on my holiday bonus.

"They gave me a lousy two hundred fifty dollars," I told him. "I'm betting three times that on football games every weekend!"

Fischel informed me he was thinking about joining an agency called Chartwell Artists, headed up by a Hollywood heavy hitter named Jerry Perenchio.

"You want me to feel him out, see if Chartwell will hire you?" Fischel asked. "I know they need a good rock guy."

"These fuckers I work for, Don, they're all mobbed up, you know that," I said. "I try to leave, I wind up at the bottom of Santa Monica Bay."

I was only half kidding. I knew I didn't want to get on the wrong side of Sidney Korshak. But I also knew that Perenchio, an old-school MCA guy who repped people like Liz Taylor, Richard Burton, Andy Williams, Glen Campbell, Henry Mancini, and Johnny Mathis, had plenty of juice himself.

If I was going to jump ship at Associated, I wanted to go out on top. At the Newport Pop Festival at Devonshire Downs, in the Valley, I repped maybe half the acts on the bill, including Creedence, the Rascals, Eric Burdon, Canned Heat, and Ike and Tina, fitting into a lineup that also featured Jimi Hendrix, Jethro Tull, the Byrds, and Johnny Winter. For three days in June 1969, 150,000 total fans jammed into a sweltering landscape that resembled not at all the "downs" of the Devonshire countryside.

I stood backstage, a tent of canvas between me and the blistering sun, and looked out over the crowd of postadolescent lobsters shrieking Jimi Hendrix's name.

"Jeee-meeee!"

Creedence, the band that I had brought into Associated, was slated to go on after Hendrix. My bitterness at my bosses at Associated boiled over. Here I was, standing before a huge audience, at the top of my game. Associated was going to be sorry to see me go.

Two-hundred-and-fifty-dollar holiday bonus *this*, motherfuckers.

Some Hell's Angels loitered behind the stage area, telling people they were going to head up on stage and that nobody was going to stop them. The disaster of Altamont was six months in the future, so the Angels still weren't linked with death at music festivals yet, but I knew I didn't want a gang of bikers bumming everybody out.

Me with Steve Gold, manager of War and Eric Burdon

"Those assholes try to get up onstage, toss 'em off," I told a burly security guard. "Anybody wearing a chain comes near here, kick their ass."

Which the security guard proceeded to do. When the Hell's Angels rushed the stage, he picked up the lead biker and tossed him down a metal stairway, knocking the others over like a set of bowling pins.

That security guard's name was Dick Griffey, who I would later have to deal with as the head of S.O.L.A.R. Records and the confidant to Suge Knight. Dick and I went a long way back, to the days he booked R&B shows. He was a pretty good security guard, though, and maybe he should have stayed just like he was on that hot afternoon at Devonshire Downs: a biker ass-kicker.

I turned to see Hendrix and his Band of Gypsys drummer (and future California Raisins lead singer) Buddy Miles exit their limousine together. Both of them had blood running down their arms.

Not long for the world, I thought. I was right about Jimi, but wrong about Buddy.

Terry Ellis, Jethro Tull's manager, approached me. He was wearing the same style of pink button-down I'd seen him in at the Fillmore.

"You've got to do something for me," Ellis said. He and his partner Chris Wright combined their two names to come up with Chrysalis Records (Chris Ellis), and had signed monster British rock acts such as Tull and Ten Years After.

"I know that Fogerty and Creedence are going on soon," Ellis said. "And Jethro Tull doesn't go on until after them. But if Fogerty goes on now, then everybody will leave. Tull will be playing to an empty field. Please, man, let us go on first. This gig is everything for us."

It was an age when playing for 150,000 people at a music festival could be enough to break an act.

"I don't have that kind of control over John Fogerty," I said. Which was true. Fogerty was always very much his own guy. Of all the people I've ever represented, I can pick out two who could have taken care of the business end themselves—management, booking, everything. Those two were John Fogerty and Elton John. They were both that savvy.

Bobby Gibson, the press agent for Tull and a drinking buddy of mine, began to tug on my sleeve too. "Please, man, come on, do it for the kid."

"I'll talk to John," I said.

"All right!" Gibson and Ellis said together.

I went to Creedence's tent and spoke to John Fogerty, not about Tull, but about our business relationship in general. I was leaving Associated, I told him. I didn't ask him to come along with me to Jerry Perenchio's Chartwell Artists. I didn't poach or pressure him in any way. But I did keep him tied up long enough for Ian Anderson and Jethro Tull to hit the stage and do their thirty minute act.

It was Tull's first major U.S. tour. Devonshire was their big break. They blew up huge after that. John Fogerty didn't appreciate the fact that I had sandbagged him. And suddenly I found myself exactly where I didn't want to be—on the wrong side of the mobsters who ran Associated Booking.

After Devonshire Downs, I rode up in the elevator with Bobby Phillips. I told him I was leaving the agency to go with Perenchio, but that I'd stay around for a couple of weeks of transition if he wanted me to.

"You have five minutes to get the fuck out of the office,"

Phillips snarled. "Make sure you leave your Rolodex."

In those days, the small-shop independent agents had an unwritten nonpoaching rule. It was very much okay to steal clients from the big guys, from Ashley/Famous Agency or William Morris or ICM. But the single-office agencies generally agreed to leave each other's clients alone. Otherwise there would have been blood all over Sunset Boulevard.

I got home that night to my Sunset Strip apartment, only to be woken up at three a.m. by a phone call. No one on the line, just breathing and then a hang-up click. I tried to go back to sleep, and a half hour later it happened again.

Sidney Korshak calling. Not the Man himself, of course— one of his guys.

I was scared. I was twenty-nine years old, an age I thought would be obscene if it were carved into my tombstone. I cussed myself out for ever speaking to John Fogerty. What was I thinking? That no one would notice? I didn't go into work at Associated. I called the phone company and got a new, unlisted number. I thought that would put me beyond Associated's reach.

At three a.m. the night after I got my new phone number, the phone rang again. When the Mob wants to get to you, they'll get to you, whether you're unlisted or not.

The message was clear. You leave us, you're not taking John Fogerty or the Rascals. You are not taking anything you didn't come in with. Count yourself lucky at that.

I did.

VI

It's official. Andrew Jerrold Perenchio, partner with Norman "All in the Family" Lear, past owner of Oak Communications cable company, current owner of Spanish TV powerhouse Univision, is now richer than God.

When I worked for him at Chartwell Artists in the early 1970s, Jerry Perenchio was already a heavy hitter. You can't have a client list studded with the biggest names in the music and movie business and not be a mover and shaker. And I was the designated young Turk who was going to drag Chartwell kicking and screaming into the brave new world of rock and roll.

To get to know my new boss, I took Perenchio and his fiancée, Jackie Thaxton, along with me one night as I made my rounds on the Strip. I wanted them to see my biggest act, Lee Michaels, a stomp-rocker who was the king of the West Coast back then, with songs such as "Keep the Circle Turning" and "Do You Know What I Mean?"

Michaels was playing at my home away from home, Elmer Valentine and Mario Maglieri's Whisky A Go-Go. The Whisky was the birthplace of the go-go girl. It earned its name at a show by Strip regular Johnny Rivers, when a female DJ in the sound booth cage got so excited that she leaped up and started dancing. The crowd loved it, and Mario and Elmer kept the go-go girl as part of their shows.

My idea of a perfect night was to hit the first show at the Whisky, where the house band was likely to be a little quartet called the Doors, or a brass-and-rock act called Chicago. Then I'd roll next door to Sneaky Pete's, the best steakhouse in the known universe.

Sneaky Pete's was my place. I was a regular, which granted

me certain privileges. I recall entering Pete's one evening, when sitting at the bar waiting for tables were Johnny Carson, Ed McMahon, John Wayne, and Glen Campbell. I walked in just as a table opened, and maître d' Joe Howard swept me past them all and seated me immediately. Of course, that didn't mean I was bigger or more important than those superstars. It just meant I went to Sneaky Pete's every single night, at times also bringing my acts along and spending my expense-account dollars.

After dinner I'd roll back next door for the second show at the Whisky. Then I'd proceed down the Strip, hitting the Roxy, say, or the Kaleidoscope or the Troub, or just hang outside and get a contact high from all the cannabis in the air. That was my routine.

Lee Michaels at the Whisky A Go-Go represented a painful auricular experience. He played a souped-up Hammond B3 organ that was the loudest instrument known to man. That evening, as Michaels had his Hammond in full roar, I glanced over at Perenchio and his soon-to-be wife. She was nodding along with the howitzer of sound. But he had his fingers stuffed in his ears.

Jerry's new wife, Jackie, played a crucial role in what was perhaps the apogee of my early career as an agent, which was bringing Elton John to the States for his first American appearances. She was my only ally at the agency, the only one who believed in Elton as much as I did.

"This guy's going to be the biggest star in the world," I told Perenchio, although I could already see he wasn't buying it. But sometimes the boss's wife can be a better ace in the hole than any coworker or associate.

I met Elton in England when he was already making a name for himself there. The first time I went out with him socially, he took me to the Speakeasy Club in a narrow London lane—so narrow that someone dinged my limousine while we were there. The club was one frequented by the real powers behind the throne of rock: the roadies. It was a club where all of England's roadies used to hang out, so of course a lot of big-name musicians went there too. Elton and I met up with Eric Clapton, and Jeff Beck came in and sat down with us. That's the kind of company Elton was keeping, even though he was still an unknown in the States.

Beck said to Clapton, "Hey, Eric, you know something, man? I think we'd better find a new line of work."

"What do you mean?" old Slowhand said. Just two guitar gods talking.

"I heard a guy yesterday who will change the way people think about what we do," Beck said. "His name is Jimi Hendrix."

Meanwhile, I thought Elton was a guy who might change the way everyone thought about pop music, and I was itching to bring him to America. I booked him for six nights at Doug Weston's club, the Troubadour, in August 1970.

I have a collection of magical moments in music—shows that demonstrate the transcendence that music can help an audience achieve. Otis Redding at Monterey was one. You can't watch a foreign movie without subtitles and hope to understand it. Yet anyone in the world, English-speaker or not, could grasp Otis's message on that stage in Monterey. Music is the ultimate form of communication.

Elton John gave me one of those moments—two, actually:

one opening night at the Troubadour, and one the weekend before his gig. I asked him to play a casual set at producer Peter Asher's house. Asher had a mansion in Hancock Park, the old-money part of L.A., which he was able to buy because of his phenomenal success as one half of the sixties pop duo, Peter and Gordon. As the older brother of Paul McCartney's girlfriend Jane Asher, Peter had access to the Beatles' song catalog, and scored a number-one hit with Lennon and McCartney's "World Without Love."

Asher had gone on from there to become one of the top music producers in the world, his services in high demand. So he was able to invite quite a crowd of music people to this intimate afternoon featuring a new singer from across the Atlantic. James Taylor showed up, and his sister Kate. Elton and his bandmates were eager to go because Asher had a swimming pool in his backyard, and these British guys had rarely encountered that luxury before.

We never made it into the pool. Elton played for hours that hot afternoon, just him at Peter Asher's baby grand. I saw him put a spell on a group of jaded industry types that no one wanted to break. He played songs he cowrote with Bernie Taupin, who was right there with him: "Your Song," "Take Me to the Pilot," "Bad Side of the Moon," as well as a smashing cover of "I've Been Loving You Too Long." That night I knew I had been right about Elton. He was a superstar.

He proved it again during his run at the Troubadour. Word gets out in the music community as if by telepathy, and everyone showed up at those shows, from Quincy Jones to Leon Russell. I called up Bill Graham, babbling, midshow on the first night.

"Bill, man, I have just seen the future of music!" I shouted into the phone, high on life and on Elton's songs. "You've got to book this guy!"

At the close of Elton's run, I hosted a small party at my Benedict Canyon house. Most of the partyers congregated in the master bedroom on the first floor, which had massive floor-to-ceiling gray-washed doors that opened out onto a lemon orchard.

Whoever wasn't in the bedroom was down in the wine cellar, where I stored a thousand bottles of expensive *premiere crus*. Some of the guys had locked themselves in down there and were getting screaming loud drunk. They took to smashing the necks off my precious French reds, one after another. It made me insane, but there was nothing I could do. Bobby Gibson, Elton's publicist, had taken the key into the cellar with him, and partied down with revelers such as Journey drummer Aynsley Dunbar and Hugh Maskela's trombone player and manager Stu Levine.

The party was rapidly slipping out of control. All week long Doug Weston had been dogging me, trying to get me to sign an option agreement stating that Elton would play at Weston's club in San Francisco and future dates in Los Angeles. Not wanting to lock Elton in, and having my eye on Bill Graham's Fillmore instead, I avoided Weston all week.

He was a hard guy to avoid, towering over nearly everyone at six seven, with stringy blond hair and round, wire-rim glasses. He ran with a group of wild men, big and crazy and always high, whom I dubbed "the alternative mafia." They weren't Sicilian but acted as if they were. When Weston pulled up in front in a Lincoln Town Car and left the motor running as if for a fast getaway, I sent Elton out the back way and prepared to face Weston.

Doug didn't disappoint. He walked into the party with an eleven-inch bowie knife strapped to his leg. A lot of hippies wore knives back then, but with Weston you got the idea the blade had just been freshly used, probably to disembowel an agent.

"You didn't invite me to your party," Weston said menacingly. "How could you have a party and not invite me?"

I told him I had posted a notice about the party in the Troubadour kitchen.

"You should have invited me personally," he said. Then he pulled out his big Bowie and began cleaning his nails with it.

Jack Kellman, my faithful running buddy, edged over to back me up. I could tell what he was thinking. In the bureau behind us I always kept a replica Luger.

Weston babbled about signing Elton to the option contract, getting crazier and crazier, practically frothing at the mouth. He stripped to the waist and began doing some sort of wild dance with his bowie-knife battle-ax. I couldn't believe what I was seeing.

Kellman slid his hand into the bureau and pulled out the Luger replica. The gun looked like the real thing, but it was actually a BB gun, and when Jack tilted it forward to point it at Doug, I could clearly hear the copper BBs roll forward in the barrel.

This isn't going to work, I said to myself. But magically, it did. I've always had a reputation for being a hard-ass who keeps a lot of guns around, and I guess it paid off then, because the half-naked Weston fled. He dove into his getaway car and roared off down Benedict Canyon.

I was glad Elton hadn't been there to see contract negotiation, American style. Eventually, I hied him out of town to a gig
on the Hawaiian Islands. I took him to Hawaiian Imperial
Hotel, where they had a place called the Second Floor, a very
fancy restaurant, and a nightclub called the Third Story.

Elton had played a triumphant show that night at the
Honolulu Convention Center, and the owners of the Third
Story cajoled him into getting up onstage. I was so drunk that I
joined the band onstage. Elton tossed me a tambourine to keep
me occupied, but after a couple of songs he came over and took
the tambourine away from me.

"Jerry," he laughed, "you're the only man I've ever met in my
life who can't keep time on a tambourine."

Elton was the kind of transcendent talent that puts him in a
whole other league, in a group of superstars I've always thought
of as the "overs." The term comes from sports betting, where
you place wagers on whether the total score in a contest will be
over or under a certain figure. You can bet the overs, or bet the
unders.

Bobby Gibson, Elton's publicist, was with me the night the
reference was coined. We spent a celebratory night at another
of my favorite watering holes, the Palm steakhouse in Los
Angeles.

RESTAURANTS I HAVE KNOWN AND LOVED: PART THREE

Wally Ganzi and Bruce Bozzi took over from their fathers at the
first Palm steakhouse in New York, at Forty-fifth Street and
Second Avenue. Then they opened another one across the
street, calling it Palm Too. There are twenty-five Palms all over

the world now, but the one I know and love, the one with my caricature painted on the wall ("Palm Lobster #1 with a Bullet") right above Irving Azoff and Bob Krasnow, is in Los Angeles, on Santa Monica Boulevard.

When I was a regular at the Palm in the 1970s, there might have been a few people who could have gotten a booth ahead of me—maybe Dodger pitcher Sandy Koufax and New York Jets quarterback Joe Namath, one or two others—but there weren't many. It was my place. Wally Ganzi hired an impeccable maître d' named Gigi Delamaestro, a small muscular guy with a big mustache, the kind of maître d' who'd get insulted if you tried to tip him, as though he were an owner, which he probably was.

The night Gigi Delamaestro gave me the expression "unders and overs," I was in the Palm with Gibson. A dozen obnoxious middle-aged Texans, all drunk as lords, lit up cigars after their meal. They were beefy ex-jock types, and their wives looked like Vegas showgirls, hard and brassy and loud.

Gigi went to their table and asked the Texans to put out their cigars. The guys languidly complied, but their wives lit into Gigi as though he were a peasant.

"You know who we are?" one of the wives shrieked. "We're running a five-thousand-dollar check here." The wives loudly informed Gigi that their husbands were the biggest beer distributors in all of Texas.

Accepting that fact for what it was worth, Gigi stepped away from the table and resumed his duties at the door. We were great friends, and whenever he could he walked over to where I sat at the bar and we kibitzed a while.

Then the Texans lit up their cigars again.

The five-foot-five Gigi stepped over and said, "I told you

before—your cigars bother my other customers. Put them out now." He was more curt than he had been the first time. When he walked back to me at the bar, five of the women followed him, all six-foot-tall bottle-blond harridans. They crowded around little Gigi, yelling at the top of their quite generous lungs.

"I don't know who you think you are talking to, little man," one of harridans screamed. "You've got a lot of nerve; who the fuck do you think you are? You know there isn't a guy at that table who makes less that five hundred thousand dollars a year."

Gigi looked up at her. "Honey," he said, "in this place, that's the unders."

With that, I jumped off the barstool, elbowed two of the women aside, grabbed Gigi and kissed him on the forehead. What a fucking put-down! And he was right. The room was full of dozens of heavyweights who could easily out-hit the Texans.

"I have never heard anything like that in my life," I crowed to Gigi. "I will immortalize you, man. I'm gonna tell this story one million times, and every time I tell it, I am going to give you credit." I'm keeping my promise here. Rest in peace, little man.

The overs and the unders, honey. Talent, money, love, whatever you have, if you've got enough of it, you're in with the overs. Gibson and I embraced that concept and started using it instantly, right there at the bar of the Palm.

"Our guy, Elton John, definitely one of the overs," I assured him.

"Otis Redding, man," Gibson said, "he was over the fucking overs."

The world is divided into two kinds of people, those who divide the world into two kinds of people and those who don't.

I've always tried to take everyone as they come and not get into placing too many judgments. But deep in my secret heart I'm placing my bets. Overs or unders.

I rolled out of the Palm that night, slept off the Vitamin V the next day, and journeyed north to Marin County, to meet one of the great overs of all time.

VII

A fable of the early 1970s: At the end of Spring Valley

Road in Marin County, California, lived a violinist and singer named Janet Planet, with her beau, an ornery Rumpelstiltskin in a three-piece suit. Rumpelstiltskin possessed one of the greatest, most powerful singing voices ever heard, and had songwriting talents to boot, but he was so nasty that a lot of people refused to work with him.

That's when I came along to save the violinist from penury and liberate the ornery singer from the prison of his own negativity.

And we all lived happily ever after.

Well, okay, not quite. At the end of 1972 I did indeed journey to the end of that dirt road in Fairfax, just north of San Francisco in Marin County. And Van Morrison's wife at the time was indeed named Janet Planet, and she was having a difficult time with her husband. Saddled with a curious mixture of stage fright and arrogance, Morrison had burned a lot of bridges in the music world, especially among agents and promoters, by not showing up at concerts.

"I dig singing the songs," Morrison said. "But there are times when it's pretty agonizing for me to be out there."

Just as agonizing as it was for promoters *not* to have him out there. The country star George Jones has a song called "No Show Jones," which parodies his own propensity for skipping dates, but there is no more serious sin that a performer can commit. The repercussions ripple through the whole music hierarchy, from the impresario who has put up money to rent the hall, down to the sound crew and ticket takers, and finally to the fans who get burned. Once you have a reputation as a canceler of shows, it's like the mark of Cain, almost impossible to remove.

Van the Man

Morrison and his spectacular ex-agent Peter Golden at William Morris had split because Van was canceling concerts left and right. But I had a reputation of being able to handle difficult acts. Once again, I was put in touch with Van by Freddie Gershon, the same lawyer who would hook me up with Springsteen a few years later.

Why did I go to the ends of the earth—or at least to the end of that dirt road—to pursue George Ivan "Van the Man" Morrison? Two reasons. One was that I knew him to be a modern master. Every musician I knew had literally worn out the grooves on Morrison's album *Astral Weeks*. They played the record so much it wouldn't play anymore, and they were forced to go out and buy another copy.

The second reason was that, professionally speaking, I had vaulted off into the unknown. With my coworker Don Fischel, I left the world of Chartwell behind to form our own independent agency. Heller-Fischel. "Est. 1970 to serve the personalized needs of a limited number of artists" was our motto. We hoped it didn't become too much a self-fulfilling prophecy, and our client list wouldn't get *too* limited.

So I was on the lookout for new acts to sign. Van Morrison wasn't a new act, of course, but he had developed a reputation, not only as a no-show, but as a very difficult man to deal with. We were two people of vastly different backgrounds, with different educations and taste, but we had one thing in common: We both liked what he did.

I liked what Van Morrison did quite a lot. I wore out my own copy of *Astral Weeks*. That was enough to get me up to Marin County. I visited the sound studio first, a two-floor affair where the control room overlooked the darkened space where Van sang. After hearing this incredible, glorious voice, I experienced an abrupt disconnect seeing a stumpy Irishman in a three-piece corduroy suit step out of the studio. It was like seeing a clown step out of the winning car at the Indianapolis 500.

I knew about Van and Janet's house in Fairfax because Lee Michaels lived in Marin too. Lee had a beautiful three-acre estate, where he kept cheetahs and bobcats as pets. He married Mary Hughes, the long-haired blond girl in all the Beach Party movies.

All of which gave me an opening with Mrs. Van Morrison, aka Janet Minto, aka the "Brown-Eyed Girl," aka Janet Planet. "Do you see what Mary Hughes drives?" I asked her. "A Mercedes convertible. Have you ever been over to the Michaels's house? A very nice place, don't you think?"

When you can't appeal to reason, appeal to the pocketbook. "Wouldn't you like to drive a nice car and afford to make a few changes to this place?"

Actually, Van and Janet's house was very funky, on a nice piece of property but basically a log cabin. I knew that homeowners were forever wishing to have things a little different, to remodel just a little bit more. I spoke to Janet about private schools for the kids. Vacations. Shopping. All the things money can buy.

"Look, Janet, I'll book Van in a heartbeat, and I know there are legions of fans out there who would love to see him live. But I have to have your promise on something before I do that. You have to keep him on tour. You have to be able to keep him sober and on the road. Can you do that?"

Visions of sugar-plum Mercedes and redecorated bathrooms dancing in her head, Janet Planet told me that yes, she could keep Van on tour. And she did better than that. She hired two friends and the three of them worked as Van's backup singers.

So we were off to the races. Heller-Fischel had its first

superstar client, and Van Morrison headed out on tour to face his fears.

He was fantastic. After the second date, a triumphant concert at the Santa Monica Civic Auditorium, I threw Van and Janet a party at the Rainbow on the Strip. All of rock royalty was there, including a strange androgynous singer who had not quite been elevated to the throne, David Bowie. Seared into my memory of the party was not the usual decadent circus of Mario's Rainbow, but an outlandish suggestion that my buddy "Miami" Mike Gruber made to Bowie that night.

"Let's go over and talk to David," Gruber said to me. "I met him once with Jagger." Gruber was the ultimate music insider, the former Rolling Stones "recreational consultant," responsible for partying and shopping. I knew Bowie from when I booked him to open on a tour with the Guess Who. He and his entourage were as surreal as human beings could possibly be. I hesitated to venture into their dressing rooms, not knowing what I might find.

Miami Mike and I staggered over to say hello to Bowie, who sat alone in a booth book-ended by two bodyguards, one black one white. This was around the time of Ziggy Stardust, when he was on the cusp of full-blown fame.

"David, I've got a great idea for your next tour," Miami Mike said, with all the enthusiasm that four or five vodkas can summon. "I know a plastic surgeon, Dr. Lake, and what we do is go to him before your next tour and have him implant a couple of boobs on you. Then you do the whole tour in a sexy blue cocktail dress."

Fucked up as I was, I still couldn't believe what I was hearing. More fantastic than what Gruber was babbling on about was the fact that Bowie was nodding along, seriously considering the prospect of owning a pair of 34DDs.

"Then, after the tour," Miami Mike continued, "if you decide you don't like them, we can always go back to Dr. Lake and have him take them out."

Bowie nodded. The two bodyguards nodded. I just shook my head.

David never got around to following Gruber's suggestion, but he did manage to tread the gender borderline very artfully, becoming a superstar in the process.

After the Santa Monica date and the Rainbow party, the Van Morrison tour ran into a snag.

"I don't care what you say, I'm not playing New York," he said immediately after looking at the list of venues I typed up. "They booed me there last time."

"Come on, man, you have to play the city—that's Ron Delsener territory, and he's the greatest showman on the face of the planet next to Bill Graham."

Ron Delsener was way up there on my list of all-time great promoters. He was a frustrated stand-up comic. Whenever you called him, you listened to ten minutes straight of really funny stand-up comedy before he would let you get down to business.

But neither Ron's reputation nor his comedy schtick could sway Van. He refused to play New York.

We embarked on the tour without firming up the Delsener date at Carnegie Hall. Van did well. He had a problem making eye contact with his audience. If he caught someone's eye, it tended to throw him off stride, so he wore dark Ray Charles–style glasses on stage. The fans were so jubilant hearing his great songs sung in his superb Irish voice that most of them were goggle-eyed anyway.

We had hit Boston, and Ron Delsener was calling me every

ten minutes, saying we would have to cancel and give the money back if Morrison wasn't going to do the show. Ron was desperate.

What is a tour? I remember asking myself. *You land at an airport. All airports look the same. You drive in a limousine. All limousines look the same. You stay in a hotel room. All hotel rooms look the same. You show up in the green room. All green rooms look the same.*

Were we in New York? Boston? Philadelphia? Maybe Van Morrison wouldn't notice the difference.

It was an outlandish thought, but I took Ronnie's next call and told him that, yes, Van Morrison would play Carnegie Hall.

Touring is blood rushing around the body electric. I've always lived my professional life not centered around the record release but around the tour date. When artists face their public, some of them react as though they are facing the firing squad. No to the blindfold, yes to the cigarette. But my great expertise was always putting together bills that would work out on the road. I was an expert at combinations where the whole added up to more than the sum of the parts, where two plus two equaled five.

I once booked a tour that put three up-and-coming bands on the same bill: Electric Light Orchestra, Journey, and Little Feat. That tour sold out every show, with groups that would have had difficulty filling even midlevel venues alone. It worked because of how the bands played off each other.

Bert Jacobs was one of the great managers, who handled Three Dog Night and Steppenwolf. He had coke bottle glasses and a wig that sat a little askew on his head. Somewhere in his past he had been a huge bookmaker, and always boasted that he was the guy behind the City College of New York point-shaving scandal back in the fifties.

Jacobs had people in his office who seemed to do nothing but roll joints all day long. Breakfast joints, before-lunch joints, dinner joints, joints for sex.

"The thing I admire about you, Jerry," Jacobs once said to me, "is that you are the man with the two hundred IQ. But somehow you've figured out what other smart guys can't figure out, which is how not to outsmart yourself."

The subtle warning of Bert Jacobs came back to me as I landed with Van Morrison at LaGuardia. I kept waiting for Rumpelstiltskin to wake up to his surroundings. I had fudged the specifics of the show to Van the Man. If this is Thursday, this must be Philadelphia.

March 18, 1972. Off in the distance as we left the plane in Queens, I could clearly see the distinctive skyline of New York City, the ill-fated World Trade Center towers and the beacon of the Empire State Building.

I have finally managed to outsmart myself, I thought, remembering Bert Jacobs's words. Van Morrison would react with rage when he realized where we were, call Freddie the Lawyer to fire my ass, never talk to me again.

But it didn't happen. A sleepy-lidded Van merely ducked into the back of the limo with nary a look around. He slumped in the backseat, exhausted and dull-eyed, for the whole ride into the city. He didn't notice anything. He was in that curious state of suspended animation called being on tour.

Someone else handled the sound check. Morrison strode out onto the stage at Carnegie Hall and did three songs to a wildly applauding audience without knowing exactly where he was.

After the third song, he asked for the house lights. *Uh-oh,* I thought. The jig was up. He examined the venue and knew he was playing Carnegie Hall. And when he heard the wild roar of applause from the New York audience, he realized he didn't have to worry about getting booed by a Bronx cheer or a Manhattan raspberry ever again.

He tore off his dark glasses and threw them into the audience. Then he kicked into "Brown-Eyed Girl." At that moment the crowd got lifted to a whole other plane. We weren't in New York after all. We had been transported to Van-Land.

Otis at Monterey. Elton at Peter Asher's house and the Troubadour. And Van Morrison at Carnegie Hall. My magical musical moments. Because Van Morrison played a great show that night, a show that justified all my ridiculous subterfuge, a show that actually helped justify my whole life in music.

Concerts at Carnegie were governed by strict union rules which required massive outlays of money for each hour of overtime. If a concert ran long, the promoter—in this case, Ronny Delsener—was the one who suffered.

Van Morrison ran long that night.

I turned to Delsener back stage. "I'm sorry, Ronny," I said. "You want me to get him off?"

"It's on me," Delsener said. The New York concert dodge is notoriously competitive, with razor-sharp profit margins. Having Ronny Delsener offer to pay overtime is something that just never happened.

"It's on me," he said again, and we both turned back to the stage to watch Van perform the third of his eight encores. Two business guys, turning around to watch the show.

Show business. Two words.

REAL NIGGAZ DON'T DIE

The test is the same, but the answers always change

I

As soon as Cube and Dre left Ruthless, they unloaded on Eazy as if they were dump trucks, one dis track after another. I know there's a long-standing custom of "snaps" (snappy comebacks) or "the dozens" in African-American culture, an insult tradition that writer Mike Davis identified as "self-loathing raised to a tribal imperative." But tradition or not, it hurt me to see my friend Eazy endure the slurs of his former bandmates.

> *You're gettin' fucked real quick,*
> *And Eazy's dick is smellin' like MC Ren's shit . . .*
> *But if they were smart as me*
> *Eazy-E would be hangin' from a tree*

It's hard to decide what's more degrading, Cube's phobic preoccupation with describing gay sex, or his willingness to adopt the role of a Klan-style lynch-man (he even named his crew the Lench Mob). But I guess identifying with the

Eazy in a rare phoneless, contemplative moment, with Mike Klein in the background

oppressor is one of the tragedies of the oppressed.

Whatever the psychology behind it, Cube and Dre's defections left Eazy feeling under siege. Especially after Dre's masterwork, *The Chronic*, came out the day after Christmas in 1992, Eazy felt he needed to show the world that Ruthless was not dependent on the two turncoats who had left it.

Oddly, *The Chronic* put a lot of money in Eazy's pocket. After Dre left N.W.A., I met with Dre's new music-business rabbi, Jimmy Iovine, at Interscope's offices in Westwood. Iovine desperately wanted Dre and Suge Knight's Death Row Records under Interscope's wing.

"I don't want to buy a lawsuit from you," Jimmy said to me. "But I have to tell you, man, Dre says he is never going to record for you again."

We hammered out a deal. Interscope would honor Dre's contract by paying Ruthless 10 percent of all monies he gained by producing, and 15 percent of those gained by his own records, with a huge advance from Interscope for agreeing to free up Eazy's former bandmate.

The deal would lead to some odd circumstances. On *The Chronic*, Dre mounted a vicious attack against Eazy, me, and Ruthless. "Dre Day" was a dis song to end all dis songs. But I think Eazy had the last laugh, since he was getting 15 percent of "Dre Day," the very song that attacked him.

As *The Chronic* hit number one, Dre gloated. He was quoted in the press as saying, "I guess Jerry picked the wrong nigga."

Well, Andre, you're right. You've made millions of dollars since you left N.W.A. (You could have made much more, but that's another subject.) The acts you've produced have grossed billions. Eazy-E couldn't come close, so in a sense you were right, he was the "wrong" guy.

But he was the guy I started with. The concept of loyalty, what political consultant James Carville called "stickin'," was important to me. Dre may have thought he was the wrong dude, but Eazy was who I went to the party with, so that's all I have to know.

Dre himself picked the "wrong" guy too, because soon enough his alliance with Suge Knight turned sour, as I always knew it would. Dre skulked away from Death Row Records. He says he left with plenty, but his half of the company and the masters remained behind. Maybe Eazy-E was the "right nigga" for Dre after all.

None of it mattered to Eric. For a while he was desperate to prove Ruthless was more than what Dre and Cube had brought to it. He would sign anyone who said they were about to sign with Dre. Our old "one record at a time" philosophy fell by the way-side. In the wake of *The Chronic*, Eazy and I juggled twenty-nine separate, simultaneous projects at Ruthless. It was insane.

Even before Dre left, we had developed Blood of Abraham, a Jewish rap group. Their featured song was called "Niggaz and Jewz (Some Say Kikes)." There was also a sexy girl group called H.W.A.—"Hos with Attitude." Eric used to unleash H.W.A. on record executives and instruct the girls to "Sharon Stone those motherfuckers," referring to the crotch-flashing episode in *Basic Instinct*. Above the Law turned out two more gangsta rap masterpieces, *Black Mafia Life* and *Uncle Sam's Curse*.

Blood of Abraham's production team went by the name of "Wolf and Epic," with Bret Mazur being Epic. Bret was the son of Irving Mazur, who was involved with my good friend Artie Ripp and the guys who originally discovered Billy Joel. Bret followed his dad into the music business, and Wolf and

Epic were the hottest producing team of the early 1990s.

Bret brought in a rapper named Will 1X, who came out of Tribal Nation to front a positive-vibe band called Atban, which was an acronym for A Tribe Beyond a Nation. Will 1X, aka William Adams, grew up in South Central and shared a lot of the same turf as Eazy—but their philosophies couldn't have been more different. Will connected to the peace-and-love tradition of the sixties. He was an incredible dancer, singer, musician. I always thought of him as the Paul Hornung of rap, after the triple-threat Green Bay Packer football great.

Will 1X came to Ruthless with a music video that he had done. It looked fantastic. "How much did you spend on that?" I asked him.

"I called in every favor that I had," Will said. "I think we spent a thousand dollars."

Behind Eazy's enthusiasm for the project, I bought the video for five thousand dollars and arranged in 1992 for the band to go into the studio as Will 1X and the Atban Klann. Will was one of the most talented people I have ever met, a true gentleman and a dear friend. The album was fantastic, but it never seemed to get finished. It entered that black hole that a lot of recording projects fall into.

"They ain't never going to finish that record," Eazy told me after working with Will for a year. "We got to cut them loose and let 'em go somewhere else."

So we did. Will 1X persevered. He changed his name to will.i.am and his band's name to the Black Eyed Peas. They retained the same positive vibe they threw down as Atban, and became a huge success from the late 1990s on.

Eazy had gotten himself into a frame of mind professionally wherein he could not be satisfied. He watched his former bandmates Dre and Cube release one platinum album after another. Even though Ruthless sold millions of records and continued to be a vital presence in the hip-hop world, Eazy remained sick with envy.

"Fuck those traitor motherfuckers," I told him. "We're doing fine." I regaled him with stories I had heard about Dre's misery at Death Row.

But Eazy was obsessed. He wouldn't rest until he discovered something that would put Ruthless back on top of the heap.

What he found was Bone Thugs-N-Harmony.

The group connected with Eazy while he was on a tour stop in Cleveland. I remember the call well.

"Jerry, you aren't going to believe these motherfuckers I found out here," he shouted over the phone. "They practically homeless, man, when I met them they were all hanging around a motherfucking barrel with a fire in it, trying to stay warm. You got to hear them, Jerry! Send them bus tickets and get them the fuck out there."

The group that descended upon the Ruthless offices in Woodland Hills the very next week was not a band so much as a commune, a family, a traveling circus, a rolling accident, and a state of mind: Krayzie Bone, aka Anthony Henderson, Bizzy Bone, aka Bryon McCane, Wish Bone, aka Charles Scruggs, Layzie Bone, aka, Steve Howse, and his big brother Flesh N Bone, aka Stan Howse. The Howse brothers were cousins to Wish Bone, and Mama Bone came along with the crew too.

The Bone Thugs family. "Bone," as in "joint," and they were all, Mama Bone included, the dope-smokingest beings ever to wander the earth. Luckily, Eazy, through his street connections, had access to unlimited quantities of the best smoke available.

The whole crew ate, smoked, and lived together. The Oujia

board figured prominently in their communal lives. If anyone dissed one of them, he dissed them all.

When I heard their demo tape, I knew Eazy was onto something. BTNH were different. Nothing in hip-hop had the same sound. Although they called their vocalizations "harmony," it wasn't really, not in the proper musical sense of the term, the way the Beach Boys or the Beatles sang harmony. No, what Bone did was sing in tight unison, layering their vocals into raps to give a lush, intense, choruslike sound that brought an R&B feel into hardcore hip-hop. It was irresistible.

But I was cautious. In 1993, Ruthless released a Bone Thugs-N-Harmony EP first, *Creepin On Ah Come Up*, featuring the single "Thuggish Ruggish Bone."

It hit huge. Out of car radios, on beach boomboxes, everywhere we went, all we heard was Tasha Williams (another member of the numberless Bone Thugs entourage), telling us over and over, "It's the thuggish ruggish bone."

Then Layzie came in:

You're feelin' the strength of the rump
Step up, hear the funk of the jump

"Thuggish Ruggish Bone" became *the* summer anthem of 1994. We filled out the EP with a few songs to achieve full album status; it went platinum, selling millions of units. Eazy and I hustled BTNH back into the studio, where by year's end they had turned out the best hard-core rap album since N.W.A. split up: *E. 1999 Eternal*. The rolling G-funk beats surpassed Dre's, and were the creations of DJ U-Neek and Tony C, who Eazy used at Ruthless to take up the slack after Dre left.

The Bone Thugs family may have been geniuses in the studio, but outside of it they were out of control. Gary Ballen, Mike Klein, and I were responsible for keeping the group focused and happy. A band's relationship with a record label was always a two-way street. There were obligations on both sides. My obligation at Ruthless was to make sure the Bone Thugs family didn't wind up imploding, dead, or in prison.

They didn't make it easy.

Gary Ballen and I lodged the group in motels all over the Valley, booking blocks of rooms at a time for the whole crew. After a week or so of the contained chaos that was the Bone Thugs experience, the hotel managers would inevitably eighty-six them. That happened so often that the group was eighty-sixed from every hotel along Ventura Boulevard.

"Now these guys may be a little high-spirited," I would understate to a motel manager before checking the group in. Then I would pull out my Ruthless business card. "If you have trouble, I want to ask you a favor: Don't call the police. Please call us, instead."

We finally rented the group a place in Chatsworth, a mini-ranch in a sleepy, elderly neighborhood. One day Flesh came to me, very excited. He was a flashy guy and in his manic periods he wore a cape. This was one of those periods.

"Jerry," Flesh said. "I got an idea. I been seeing all these white people around here, just walking around, looking like they got a lot of money. What would you think if we start jacking them?"

I stared at him.

"Well, now, Flesh," I said slowly, thinking of an easy way to dissuade him. "Let's just think this through. How old are these white people you're thinking about robbing?" The streets around the Chatsworth house were filled with geriatric walkers.

"Old, fuck, real old—like they is eighty or something. They walk around like in jogging suits. I could take 'em, easy."

I told him that eighty-year-olds in jogging outfits probably weren't carrying too much money on them. Reluctantly, he gave up his plan.

With BTNH, minor difficulties had a way of turning into major disasters. The whole Bone Thugs family traipsed into a Wells Fargo branch in Woodland Hills to cash a six-figure check—they always called their royalty payments their "cheese."

"We're going down to Wells Fargo," Bizzy Bone announced when I slid the Ruthless check across my desk to him. "I want my cheese."

An elderly woman in a house across the street saw a group of African-American males wearing watch-caps enter a bank. That was enough for her: She called the cops to report a bank robbery in progress. The ensuing uproar cost Ruthless one hundred thousand dollars to straighten out. Not their fault, of course, but events always seemed to topple into chaos when the group was around.

After the raging success of "Thuggish Ruggish Bone," we went back and forth on the amount of an advance Ruthless would pay for the group's album—the record that would become their masterpiece, *E. 1999 Eternal*.

In negotiations, I always start quoting a low offer, knowing it's not a position I can necessarily sustain. Advances were pure mathematics, formulated by judging how much we thought the album would sell. I offered BTNH a $225,000 advance.

Bizzy, one of the major figures in the group, leaped immediately to his feet. "You're not going to give us our cheese, man! I'm out of here!"

It was so obviously a rehearsed move that I almost laughed out loud. I was very fond of Bizzy. He went out to the hall and made a big show of getting on his cell phone. He wanted me to think he was calling a competing label, maybe Jimmy Iovine or Doug Morris, but I knew he was probably only talking to one of his girlfriends.

Layzie, the de facto head of the group, stayed behind.

"We want four-fifty," he informed me curtly.

Four-hundred-and-fifty-thousand dollars was precisely the number I had in mind when we started this fandango. I knew Layzie had merely taken my offer and doubled it. From that point on I learned to offer the Bone Thugs family half of what I actually wanted to pay. Layzie would automatically double it. So it worked out for everybody.

I had never seen Eazy happier since Dre left. "Thuggish Ruggish Bone" was putting up great sales numbers, and he knew *E. 1999 Eternal* was going to be huge when it was released. The success of BTNH legitimized Ruthless Records as a label and himself as an executive in exactly the way he craved. In Eazy's eyes, his success was an enormous "fuck you!" to Dre and Cube.

"I owe you a dinner at Monty's if that fucking record doesn't hit number one," I told Eazy, referring to *E. 1999 Eternal*. I knew that the first single we planned to release from the album, "Crossroad," would be a smash. I considered *Eternal* capable of selling fifteen million, perhaps more. I didn't think Michael Jackson's *Thriller* numbers were out of the question. *Eternal* was that good. Bone Thugs-N-Harmony would be superstars on the level of N.W.A., and Ruthless Records would reestablish its position as the premier label in hip-hop.

Fate intervened, in the form of a viral protein roughly the size of a hundred molecules of sugar, a microscopic assassin that destroyed the world of Ruthless forever.

II

All these years I've never answered the allegations of financial impropriety leveled against me, first by Cube and then by Dre. But now that I'm writing this book, I feel compelled to answer those allegations on behalf of my longtime partner, Eazy-E. This chapter's for you, little guy.

I've had to sit still and listen for two decades now to accusations from a pair of former friends and their advisors that I was a thief, a liar, and a cheat, that I was caught with my "hand in the cookie jar," that I had signed them to "draconian" contracts.

Let's take Cube first, shall we?

Cube, I'm not the master of the snap the way you are. I am not the poet laureate of rap. With all your talk about dicks-up-the-ass and lynching your former friends, you can win a freestyle battle against me any day.

I'm a numbers guy. You vocalized, I financialized. And I say to you, Cube, that the amount of money you earned at Ruthless didn't have anything to do with anyone's hand in any cookie jar. It was pure mathematics, baby—not your strong suit, from what I hear about the producers and writers you utilized at your own record label. They were screaming about not getting paid just like you used to scream. I personally would never allude to anything like that without knowing all the facts.

They may or may not have had a reason to scream. You didn't. Here are the numbers all spelled out: For every record and merchandising dollar N.W.A. brought in, Ruthless Records took twenty-five cents off the top. The label deserved it. That's a fairly conservative percentage. Ruthless sponsored your time in the studio, your tours. The label bought you your fucking pencils.

That leaves seventy-five cents to split five ways, between the five members of N.W.A., which means everyone gets fifteen cents out of every dollar.

N.W.A.'s song-publishing royalties were always hefty, because the band sold so many records. A single song on *Straight Outta Compton* might bring in one hundred thousand dollars in publishing royalties. Let's split that up dollar by dollar too, okay?

Ruthless took twenty-five cents out of each dollar of publishing royalties. Again, a fairly customary bite. Some labels take 100 percent. The other publishing companies involved (Cube's included) also took twenty-five cents. Of the fifty cents left, the lyric writer took twenty-five cents, and the beat writer took twenty-five cents. Dre composed the beats for every song N.W.A. ever put out, so he always got that quarter out of every dollar coming in, less deductions for all his sampling. You wrote a lot of the words, Cube, so some of the time you took a quarter bite out of those dollars. There were quite a few times, though, when you had to share with cowriters, such as Dre, Yella, the D.O.C., Eazy, or Ren. So sometimes you had to share your quarter.

Words and music. Lerner and Lowe, Rogers and Hammerstein.

It's not robbery. It's not a Jewish conspiracy to rip off the poor artist. What it is, O'Shea, is mathematics, pure and simple. *You received every single penny that was coming to you. If you say you didn't, then you are lying.* I don't know how to put it any clearer or any truer.

I'm tired of your slurs. It makes me sick that you exploit the anti-Semitism rampant in the world today just to justify yourself.

So here it is. I'm issuing you a challenge.

There isn't a single instance of Jerry Heller stealing, taking money under the table, cheating artists out of payments rightfully due to them. You can't do it, man. So once and for all, shut the fuck up.

Who represents you now? A Hollywood megamanagement company called the Firm, and William Morris, am I right? The guy who wrote "No Vaseline" certainly has a lot of white representatives around him now.

Cube said, "There was no way I was ever going to get paid what I was worth at Ruthless."

Okay, let's just agree that statement is true for the sake of argument. How do you get from there to rapping about the lynching of your former friend Eric Wright?

Cube claimed that, after he left Ruthless, he eventually mended fences with Eric. He spoke about a time Eric and he got together in New York City. But I know for a fact that Eric Wright never forgave O'Shea Jackson for what he perceived as ingratitude.

When you saw Eric in New York during the winter of 1994, he was playing you. Playing the playa. He never changed his mind about what a punk he thought you were. He put up a front because he wanted one thing more than any other: an N.W.A. reunion album on Ruthless Records.

Cube, this one's for the little big man. I'm answering back on behalf of Eazy. As far as you being the poet laureate of the rap generation, don't take your own hype too seriously. That tag was just something a real smart guy named Jerry Heller thought up to sell you to the public.

When Andre Young and I cross paths these days, we exchange greetings and handshakes. Everything is genial and cool. But Dre, I'm telling you right now, you were naive. Suge played you, man. All that bullshit you swallowed as the truth? None of it changed the fact that Suge was a very unpleasant guy with whom to do business, did it? When did you wake up to the reality? When did you realize you wanted to get out from under Suge's thumb? Was it worth it to sell out your friend Eazy, just to suck down a Big Gulp of Marion the Barbarian's bullshit?

You're happy now, and I'm just trifling with you. How can a man who receives a check for sixty million dollars from his record label possibly be unhappy? Except . . . what if he's worth more? It's not what you're happy with, it's what you can command in a deal.

Dre, you were always party to all contract negotiations. You even called me the "superdope manager, Jerry Heller," in one of your songs. Now you're saying, Jerry did this wrong, Jerry did that wrong. You were right there in the room! What were you doing, playing pocket pool?

If you think it was a simple achievement, in 1987, promoting a group called Niggaz With Attitude, with lyrics such as "let's get Eazy muthafukkin' E to the mike," then you should think again.

Dre, Cube—I have no animosity toward you. You made it possible for me to make millions of dollars. And you made hundreds of millions, which is the way it should be.

III

The streets aren't for dreaming now.

— TOM WAITS

Cube, Dre, Eazy—they were all dreamers. They weren't thugs. They were like the actor Robert Young: "I'm not a doctor, but I play one on TV." They played at thug life. We all laughed when Dre came out with *The Chronic* and tried to put up a thug front. Mild-mannered Andre Young! Clark Kent trying to convince you he was Lex Luthor. On "Express Yourself," he had solemnly warned kids away from drugs:

> *Yo, I don't smoke weed or sens* [sensimilla]
> *'Cause it's known to give a brother brain damage*
> *And brain damage on the mike don't manage nothin'*

A sentiment worthy of a D.A.R.E. officer. Dre was about as much of a thug as Marcus Welby, MD.

But a sea change hit the hip-hop world after Suge Knight got involved. Rap transmogrified, from artists telling stories about criminals, to the criminals themselves doing the rapping. And some of the magic went out of the music when that happened. The streets weren't for dreamers anymore.

Eric Wright had a questing, restless mind. He was always surprising me.

"I want to do a movie about the JDL," he told me shortly before his death. He always had a hundred ideas going at once. He was obsessed with the Jewish Defense League and their motto, "Never again." "Man, I can't get that out of my head," he said. "'Never again.' That's dope."

Eric caught flak for sitting in on the Simi Valley trials of the LAPD officers who beat up Rodney King. Because one of our lawyers, Harland Braun, represented one of the officers, Eric got primo seats in the gallery. So the undenied street rumor had it that Eric had come out on the side of the LAPD shit-kickers. He hadn't. He was just intensely interested in the workings of the world.

Only a handful of people were closest to Eric in the weeks leading up to his death. Toker, aka Little Beaver, his Latino street connection. The mixmaster Julio G. Mike Klein, whom Eric had promoted from security director at Ruthless to business affairs director for the label. His main girl Stephanie.

We were all fully aware of the twin obsessions that occupied Eric Wright in the fall of 1994.

One: He wanted to be in on the birth of Latino gangsta rap. Julio G, Tony G, Mellowman Ace, Frost, and Toker's group, the Brownside. Eric was convinced this music would break big. The 2005 success of Daddy Yankee and reggaeton proved him right once more.

Two: What he wanted to do more than anything else was an N.W.A. reunion album on Ruthless Records. He would have asked me to stand aside if he thought Cube and Dre wouldn't have done it with me, and I would have gladly done so—well, maybe not gladly. But I would have gotten out of the way.

As it was, I left Ruthless five weeks before Eric Wright passed away in Cedars Sinai Hospital on March 26, 1995. I couldn't stand the stench of carrion-eaters gathered around his bedside, divvying up chunks of his flesh.

It was the most horrific period of my life. I would not have survived without Gayle. She was my lifeline.

"He's not himself," I remember her telling me about Eazy, over and over. "You've got to hold on to that. Whatever he does—he's not himself."

Things fall apart. The center cannot hold. Nothing mattered to me, except the fact that Eric Wright, my best friend in the world apart from Gayle Steiner, lay dying.

The last time I saw Eric Wright, even though I didn't know it, he was already ill with the HIV virus that would kill him. He coughed like a man three times his age. His normally impeccable grooming habits had deserted him. His clothes and hair were dirty. He wasn't the Eric I knew. His clothes reeked of marijuana. Okay, well, that smell was the Eric I knew, but the rest of it showed his decline all too clearly.

We spoke about nothing personal, just Ruthless business. Show, meet business. Business, meet show.

Eric never said good-bye, ever. It was a phobia of his. He didn't this time, either.

"Jerry, we're going to need to talk some more."

"Okay," I said. "I'm around."

The last words we ever exchanged.

IV

At a press conference at the time of Eric's death, newly
appointed Ruthless lawyer Ron Sweeney read a letter from his
"dear friend" (he had represented Eric all of two-plus months)
that was supposed to represent the last "werdz" of Eazy-E.

"I may not seem like a guy you would pick to preach a ser-
mon," the statement began. "But I feel it is now time to testify."
Sweeney-as-Eric went on to say that "I just feel that I've got
thousands and thousands of young fans that have to learn about
what's real when it comes to AIDS. Like the others before me,
I would like to turn my own problem into something good that
will reach out to all my homeboys and their kin. Because I want
to save their asses before it's too late."

As soon as I heard it, I thought the letter was fake. Those
weren't his words. Deathbed confessional or not, Eric would never
have put out a letter that was that corny. Another telltale sign: In
the letter, Eric was supposed to have said, "I have seven children
by six different mothers." Eric knew full well he had eight children. He left behind three women pregnant with his children.

Church and community leaders sang Eazy's praises for the
"honesty" of that statement—a rare open acknowledgement of
AIDS by a well-known figure in the hip-hop world. I never
wanted to pop their bubble and say, look, I don't even think
Eric wrote it.

I remember what he always said. "Do I look like a motherfucking role model?"

I kept my own counsel.

For a while, I was blocked from seeing Eric's body at Angeles
Funeral Home in South Central, just as I was kept away from his
hospital room at Cedars. The same Nation of Islam bodyguards

who assumed security at the hospital had been instructed to keep me away from the funeral home. It looked as though I wasn't going to be able to pay my respects.

But then out of nowhere came K.J., Toker and the other Brownside guys who had been with me at Ruthless.

"He's getting in," K.J. said to the bow-tied Muslims. It wasn't a request. It was a statement of fact. Besides, K.J. was carrying a twelve-gauge pump-action shotgun when he said it.

Gayle and I entered the funeral home. Eazy lay dressed in an outfit that would have made him snort in derision: Pendleton-type shirt, khaki pants, doeskin work boots, a watch cap with "Compton" on it. Someone's idea of a gangbanger's outfit, but nothing that Eric would ever be, well, caught dead in. He would have worn a three-thousand-dollar three-quarter-length MCM leather jacket.

Looking at Eric Wright in death, who was always so full of life, was a surreal experience. His lips had been stitched shut. His face looked bloated and unreal, like a wax figure's. He was just thirty-one when he died.

I silently said good-bye to my friend. I was bitter that he had pushed me away during his last days. He always lived like a champ; I wish he could have gone out like one.

Then a gaggle of female teenage fans whom the guards had allowed to enter rushed in and crowded me away from the casket. "Oh, he's so cute!" they gushed. The whole scene sickened me. Gayle and I left.

Nothing mattered. Things fall apart. The center cannot hold. I watched helplessly as Ruthless Records, the huge Frankenstein's monster Eazy and I had worked so hard to create, slowly decomposed like week-old roadkill. Everything had changed. The old answers weren't good enough anymore. Formerly, I could blow through any obstacle in tandem with Eric. Now I felt as though I was back at Ohio University, sitting at the feet of Professor Homer V. Cherrington: I give the same test every year. I just change the answers.

Chemical Bank, the executor of Eazy's estate, appointed a record executive from the Warner Brothers division of black music to oversee Ruthless Records. His name was Ernie Singleton, and I knew him well from my previous years in the business. A dapper little guy, perfectly genial. But out of his milieu.

Ernie had heard somewhere about the tactic of putting his desk on a pedestal and making the chairs in his office low-slung, so whoever came in was looking up at him from a subservient position. I remember sitting in his offices at MCA. I could only see Ernie Singleton's shoes, under his desk, and his head from eye level up. The shoes were very nice affairs.

I knew Ruthless was an operation where street cred was at a premium, and Ernie's well-mannered persona didn't seem to me to fit. He had been a top exec at Warner and MCA. Putting him in as head of Ruthless Records was like hiring a guy in the GM front office to be the leader of the Chevy racing team.

Ruthless released *E. 1999 Eternal* that July. A huge success, a number-one hit, so I didn't owe Eazy a dinner at Monty's after all. But I was irritable and disamused. I thought Ruthless blew the release. "Crossroad" was put out as the album's fourth single, not the first, as I knew would have been the right move.

Ernie Singleton crowed. *Eternal* sold five million units! Huge, huge, huge! How could Chemical Bank ask for more? Everybody was happy. Except me.

Why, you dumb shits, I wanted to scream, *can't you see it? That album should have sold* five times *five million!*

I could hear the tongues wag. Oh, that Jerry Heller. He used to complain about not making more than $250,000. Now he's grousing about an album that goes platinum five times over!

Fast forward to ten years later. Bone Thugs-N-Harmony was nowhere on the charts. Ruthless sank into the ground like an old grave. Dre and Cube talked about an N.W.A. reunion every once in a while, maybe including Eric's son, the rapper L'il E, and Snoop Dogg.

"There can't be a Beatles reunion," I heard Paul McCartney say once in the 1990s, during those periodical clamors for the boys to get together again. "There can never be a Beatles reunion now, because John is dead."

Stating the obvious.

I don't have many mementos from the Ruthless years. Most of the stuff I donated to the Rock and Roll Hall of Fame in Cleveland. Recently my old friend Mark Shimmel called to ask me to be involved with the new hip-hop wing at the Smithsonian Museum. But I have kept a collection of platinum albums on the walls of my office upstairs in my house that I have no intention of parting with.

Eric Burdon once told me that in a drunken, reckless mood he broke the glass frame of a gold record he had been awarded in his Animals days. He actually managed to put the thing on his turntable and play it. Only despite what the label read ("Awarded to Eric Burdon and the Animals . . . in recognition of . . . sale of . . .") it wasn't an Animals album after all. The voice that came out of speakers was not that of Eric Burdon but of Connie Francis, from an old record of the fifties.

As Oscar Levant used to say about Hollywood, peel away the fake tinsel and you'll find the real tinsel underneath.

Eazy always told me he wanted me to have his collection of movie monster memorabilia when he died, but I never got that. I don't play the old N.W.A. albums very often. I take long walks with my beautiful wife on the tide-washed beach flats in north county San Diego, knowing that a *Baywatch* babe can always save my life if I happen to be drowning. She has saved it before.

I still have an image of Eric Wright in his glory days. Laughing, always fooling around. Happy.

Me and Lorenzo
Rolling in a Benz-o

V

Music has carried me incredible places in my life, but that general comment doesn't really get at the heart of the matter. I've talked about my magical musical moments in this book, about listening to Eazy's tape at Macola, Otis Redding at Monterey Pop, Elton John at the Troub, and Van Morrison at Carnegie Hall. I take those moments with me wherever I go. They sustain me. They represent what we are all looking for, and what music can provide: transcendence.

David Geffen called me up in the fall of 1969 to invite me to a Crosby, Stills, Nash & Young show at the Greek Theater in Griffith Park. L.A.'s usually smoggy air had been swept clean that night by warm winds off the San Gabriels, and the sky was clear. My friends and I had a box near the stage.

Jesse Colin Young and the Youngbloods opened the concert, an East Coast transplant band nurtured in the San Francisco music scene. San Francisco also nurtured folk-rocker Dino Valente of Quicksilver Messenger Service, who in the mid-sixties wrote a stirring brotherhood anthem called "Get Together."

Jefferson Airplane recorded the song first, but it wasn't until the Youngbloods did it that "Get Together" became a symbolic touchstone for a whole era. At the time of the Greek Theater concert, the Youngbloods version reigned at number one, so it was puzzling when the band did only an abbreviated version during its set. The expectation hung there, unsatisfied. Where was that song?

After the Youngbloods played that night, Joni Mitchell came out and did a short, achingly beautiful set. She was one of Geffen's up-and-coming superstars, and he knew how to vary a billing of two all-male bands with a solo female singer. David

Crosby and Graham Nash came out to start a terrific acoustic set just before intermission.

I remember Eazy's habitual attitude toward me when he knew I was going to blow him away with something: it was always as though he were standing there with his arms folded, a skeptical expression on his face, and saying, "Thrill me." He was never too impressed by anything less than the absolutely fantastic. That night in Griffith Park the whole audience got thoroughly thrilled.

The curtain opened on the second half of the show with Neil Young far up on the riser, banked behind every piece of electronic equipment known to man. Then the whole CSN&Y ensemble went electric for a rolling, soaring set that had everyone in the theater on their feet.

The evening ended under a net of California stars, with the Youngbloods, Joni Mitchell, and CSN&Y joining for an emotional, twenty-minute version of "Get Together." I let the music wash over me. I decided I loved everybody onstage, singing in perfect harmony. By the time the song ended I loved every person on Earth, every single atom in the whole damn universe.

The spirit of brotherhood had taken a few hits around that time, what with Charles Manson, Altamont, the election of Richard Nixon, and the deaths of fifty thousand young Americans in Vietnam. All the peaceful vibes of the Haight-Ashbury and the summer of love seemed to be draining away.

Yet here the spirit was, alive and well, shining in the candles and lighters audience members held aloft at the Greek Theater that night. The way Stephen Stills, Graham Nash, David Crosby, Neil Young, Joni Mitchell, Jesse Colin Young, and the others sang "Get Together" reminded me and everyone there that no matter how dark the night gets, the light shines from all of us.

I always was and still am a child of the sixties. I don't believe any form of transcendence exists, apart from music, apart from love. Both forms combined that evening in L.A., in the unforgettable performances of the musicians onstage, matched by the goodwill and warmth of the audience.

That's what music can do. That's what it's done for me, not just at specific moments, but over the course of my whole career. Right about now, I can hear Eazy saying "corny," but that's okay. I see him nodding his head and agreeing, too. I've managed to build an incredible life out of those moments, stringing them together like the beads of a hippie necklace. No one can possibly be more fortunate than that.

Calabasas and San Diego, California, March 2006

APPENDIX 1: "YOU'RE THE MAN"

I got stopped by a young, blond, buzz-cut LAPD officer as I entered the on-ramp of the 101 freeway at Haskell Avenue in Sherman Oaks.

"What'd I do wrong, officer?"

"License and registration, please."

"Okay, but what'd I do wrong?"

"You blew straight through that stop sign at the bottom of the on-ramp."

"If you said I did, then I did, because I sure didn't see it," I said. My customary on-ramp had been closed for construction, so I had been forced to take an unfamiliar one. "Look, man, I haven't gotten a traffic ticket in twenty-five years."

He looked down at me sitting in my 750il with the license plate of RTHSS II. I was wearing a yellow personalized "Baywatch Lifeguard" jacket that Gayle had given me many years before.

"Are you a lifeguard, sir?"

"My wife was an actress on *Baywatch*, and she gave me this. It's an official Santa Monica lifeguard jacket."

The cop gave me back my license and registration.

And no ticket.

"You're the man," he said, and got back on his motorcycle and roared off.

I got a big kick out of that line. I was laughing about it as I drove off. Over time I made a mental list of all the people I've known in the music business to whom I could say that three-word catchphrase:

"YOU'RE THE MAN!"

Top of the Heap

David Geffen (Could have been the best in any category; meanwhile, he was a great record executive, agent, manager, Broadway show angel, movie producer, but decided instead he'd rather be a multibillionaire entertainment mogul; as Stephen Hawking said of Einstein: "He is from a whole other planet than all the rest of us")

The Executives
Number One with a Bullet:

Clive Davis, Ahmet Ertegun, Berry Gordy Jr. (Class, style, and grace; head and shoulders above the rest of the industry in terms of longevity and accomplishments)

Way Up There:

Herb Alpert and Jerry Moss, A&M (The two best friends an artist could ever have)

Jac Holzman, Elektra (The Doors)

Chris Blackwell, Island (Bob Marley, U2)

Clive Calder, Jive (Because he sold his company for three billion dollars on the basis of *NSYNC, the Backstreet Boys, and Britney Spears)

Mo Ostin and Joe Smith, Warner (The Mo and Joe Show, and always a class act)

Doug Morris and Jimmy Iovine, Interscope, Universal Music Group (They created an unrivalled empire with a 50-plus percent market share; the most successful team of the current generation, the Doug and Jimmy Show has surpassed the Mo And Joe Show.)

Sylvia Rhone (The first female superexecutive in music)

Shoulda, Woulda, Coulda:

Bob Krasnow (Should have been even more phenomenally successful than he was)

The Managers
Number One with a Bullet:

Irving Azoff (Managed the Eagles since 1973, including the period when they sold a million records a month for twenty-nine straight months; managed Jimmy Buffet since 1975; computer model for the perfect music businessman, absolute loyalty to his clients, will kill for them, anytime, anywhere, anyplace; if I ever needed a manager, Irving would be the one I'd call)

Albert Grossman (Bob Dylan, the Band, Paul Butterfield, Janis Joplin, et al)

The team of David Geffen and Elliot Roberts

Freddie DeMann (Madonna, Michael Jackson)

Cavallo, Ruffalo and Farnoli (Earth, Wind & Fire; Prince)

Way Up There:

Jerry Weintraub (John Denver, Rick James, Pointer Sisters; produced live shows for Sinatra, Elvis, Moody Blues, and more)

One Man, One Act: Managers Steve O'Rourke (Pink Floyd), Peter Grant (Led Zeppelin), Don Hunter (The Guess Who), agent Howard Rose (Elton John)

Shoulda, Woulda, Coulda:

"Miami" Mike Gruber (Tour manager for the Rolling Stones, manager for Moby Grape, Taj Mahal, Love, etc.; decided at some point he would rather party than become a truly great manager—not that there's anything wrong with that)

Tom Hulett (A great promoter and human being, but should have stayed in Seattle instead of getting seduced by L.A.; rest in peace, my friend.)

Music Television
Number One with a Bullet:

Dick Clark (*American Bandstand*, lasted five decades in a cutthroat business and somehow always managed to stay a true gentleman)

Susan Richards (*Midnight Special*, always in the corner of the underdog, always willing to go to the wall to recognize a new act and convince Burt, Stan, Rocco, Kenny, Tisha, and Debbi)

Shoulda, Woulda, Coulda:

Don Kirschner (*Rock Concert*, great show, but it was more directed toward promoting established acts)

MTV (Thanks for banning the "Straight Outta Compton" video—it sent us on our way. What happened to you guys? Maybe you could ban my book, too?)

Promoters
Number One with a Bullet:

Bill Graham (The Fillmore East and West, Winterland; he was without a doubt the greatest impresario since P. T. Barnum)

Way Up There:

Ron Delsener (New York), Mike and Jules Belkin (Cleveland), Arnie Granat and Jerry Michaelson (Chicago), Alex Cooley and Don Fox (the South), Terry Bassett (Texas), Barry Fey (Denver), Tom Hulett (Northwest), Steve Wolf and Jim Rissmiller (Los Angeles), Tom Moffat (Hawaii) Don Law (Boston), Michael Cole (Toronto), Donald K. Donald (Montreal), Jack Boyle (D.C.), Larry Magid (Philadelphia), Irv Zuckerman (St. Louis).

Shoulda, Woulda, Coulda:

Howard Stein (Decided he'd rather be a club owner and restaurateur)

Agents
Number One with a Bullet:

Jerry Perenchio (Best in the mainstream world; the greatest dealmaker of all time; mounted the first Ali-Frazier fight with Jack Kent Cooke; sold Caesars Palace to Clifford Pearlman; promoted the Bobby Riggs-Billy Jean King tennis match; partnered with Norman Lear on such groundbreaking television as *All in the Family* and *Sanford and Son*; owned Oak Communications, Avco Embassy, Univision; at one time actually pursued plans to start his own independent municipality, like Monaco, on behalf of a couple of clients)

Frank Barsalona (Best in the rock world; represented most of the great English acts in the world)

APPENDIX 2:
A SELECT N.W.A./RUTHLESS DISCOGRAPHY

(All releases gold or platinum)

N.W.A.: *N.W.A. and the Posse* **(1987)**
1. Boyz-N-the-Hood
2. 8 Ball
3. Dunk the Funk
4. A Bitch Iz a Bitch
5. Drink It Up
6. Panic Zone
7. L.A. Is the Place
8. Dope Man
9. Tuffest Man Alive
10. Fat Girl
11. 3 the Hard Way

J.J. Fad: *Supersonic* **(1988)**
1. Supersonic
2. Way Out
3. Blame It on the Muzick
4. In the Mix
5. Eenie Meenie Beats

6. My Dope Intro
7. Let's Get Hyped
8. Now Really
9. Time Tah Get Stupid
10. Is It Love

Eazy-E: *Eazy-Duz-It* (1988)

1. Still Talkin' (Prelude)
2. Nobody Move
3. Ruthless Villain
4. 2 Hard Mutha's
5. Boyz-N-the-Hood (Remix)
6. Eazy-Duz-It
7. We Want Eazy
8. Eazy-Er Said Than Dunn
9. Radio
10. No More ?'s
11. I'mma Break It Down
12. Eazy-Chapter 8 Verse 10

N.W.A.: *Straight Outta Compton* (1988)

1. Straight Outta Compton
2. Fuck tha Police
3. Gangsta Gangsta
4. If It Ain't Ruff
5. Parental Discretion Iz Advised
6. 8 Ball (Remix)
7. Something Like That
8. Express Yourself
9. Compton's N the House (Remix)

10. I Ain't tha 1
11. Dopeman (Remix)
12. I Ain't tha 1
13. Something 2 Dance 2
14. Express Yourself (Extended Mix)
15. Bonus Beats
16. Straight Outta Compton (Extended Mix)
17. A Bitch Is a Bitch

The D.O.C.: *No One Can Do It Better* (1989)
1. It's Funky Enough
2. Mind Blowin'
3. Lend Me an Ear
4. Comm. Blues
5. Let the Bass Go
6. Beautiful But Deadly
7. The D.O.C. & The Doctor
8. No One Can Do It Better
9. Whirlwind Pyramind
10. Comm. 2
11. Formula
12. Portrait of a Master Piece
13. The Grand Finalé

Michel'le: *Michel'le* (1989)
1. No More Lies
2. Nicety
3. If?
4. Keep Watchin
5. Something in My Heart

6. 100% Woman
7. Silly Love Song
8. Never Been in Love
9. Close to Me
10. Special Thanks
11. If? (Reprise)

Above the Law: *Livin' Like Hustlers* (1990)

1. Murder Rap
2. Untouchable
3. Livin' Like Hustlers
4. Another Execution
5. Menace to Society
6. Just Kickin' Lyrics
7. Ballin'
8. Freedom of Speech
9. Flow On (Move Me No Mountain)
10. The Last Song

N.W.A.: *Efil4zaggin (Niggaz4life)* (1991)

1. Prelude
2. Real Niggaz Don't Die
3. Niggaz 4 Life
4. Protest
5. Appetite for Destruction
6. Don't Drink that Wine
7. Alwayz into Somethin'
8. Message to B.A.
9. Real Niggaz
10. To Kill A Hooker

11. One Less Bitch
12. Findum, Fuckum & Flee
13. Automobile
14. She Swallowed It
15. I'd Rather Fuck You
16. Approach to Danger
17. 1-900-2-Compton
18. The Dayz of Wayback

Bone Thugs-N-Harmony: *Creepin On Ah Come Up* (EP, 1994)

1. Intro
2. Mr. Ouija
3. Thuggish Ruggish Bone
4. No Surrender
5. Down Foe My Thang
6. Creepin on Ah Come Up
7. Foe tha Love of $
8. Moe Cheese

Bone Thugs-N-Harmony: *E. 1999 Eternal* (completed December 1994; released July 25, 1995)

1. Da Introduction
2. East 1999
3. Eternal
4. Crept and We Came
5. Down '71 (The Getaway)
6. Mr. Bill Collector
7. Budsmokers Only
8. Crossroad

9. Me Killa
10. Land of tha Heartless
11. No Shorts, No Losses
12. 1st of tha Month
13. Buddah Lovaz
14. Die Die Die
15. Mr. Ouija 2
16. Mo' Murda
17. Shotz to tha Double Glock

Eazy-E: *Str8 off tha Streetz of Muthaphukkin Compton* (1995)

1. First Power
2. Ole School Shit
3. Sorry Louie
4. Just tah Let U Know
5. Sippin on a 40
6. Nutz on Ya Chin
7. Tha Muthaphukkin Real
8. Lickin, Suckin, Phukkin
9. Hit the Hooker
10. My Baby'z Mama
11. Creep n Crawl
12. Wut Would You Do
13. Gangsta Beat 4 tha Street
14. Eternal E

INDEX

ABC/Dunhill, 243, 244
Above the Law, 171–172, 285
Adler, Lou, 242
Afrika Bambaataa, 35
Aguilera, Christina, 256
Ahlerich, Milt, 141–143, 203
Alexander, Morey, 33–34, 37, 43, 45, 46, 77, 122
Almond, Johnny, 245
"Alone Again (Naturally)," 94
Alpert, Herb, 31, 77, 308
Altamount, 258, 305
AmeriKKKa's Most Wanted (album), 183
A&M Records, 31, 77, 308
Anderson, Ian, 248–249, 261
Appel, Mike, 19
Arabian Prince (aka Kim Nazel), 67–69, 78, 97,
    103, 114
Are We There Yet? (movie), 181
Armatrading, Joan, 32, 64
Armstrong, Louis, 29, 64
Ashburne, Michael, 138
Asher, Peter, 266
Ashley Famous Agency, 251, 262
Associated Booking Company (ABC), 33,
    214–216, 222–225, 228, 238, 241, 257,
    258, 261–262
Astral Weeks (album), 275
Asylum Records, 254
Atban Klann, 286
Atco, 114–116, 148
Atlantic Records, 76, 112, 114, 115, 139, 149, 253
Audio Achievements, 69, 97–98, 103–104, 106,
    107, 109, 190
Austin, Frank, 166
"Automobile," 202
Average White Band, 249
Azoff, Irving, 60, 109, 203, 253–256, 270, 309

Baby-D (aka Dania Birks), 113
Backstreet Boys, 308

Ballen, Gary, 135, 138, 153, 156, 175, 289
Band, the, 251, 309
Barnes, Dee, 178–179
Barri, Steve, 242
Barsalona, Frank, 254, 257, 311
"Batterram," 102
Beach Boys, 64, 239, 288
"Beat It," 52
Beatles, the, 6, 30, 56, 238, 239, 288, 302
Beck, Jeff, 265
Bennett, Tony, 83
Benson, George, 32
Bernstein, Sid, 238
Biederman, Don, 244
Big Brother, 53
Big Hutch (aka Greg Hutchinson), 171, 172
Big Ron, 174–176
Big Tree, 45
Big Wes, 190–192
Biggie, 108
Birns, Alex "Shondor," 81–83, 87–88, 96, 207,
    214
"Bitch Iz a Bitch, A," 126, 173–174
Bizzy Bone (aka Byron McCane), 287, 290, 291
Black Eyed Peas, 33, 286
"Black Korea," 136
Black Mafia Live (album), 285
Black Panthers, 234–237
Blackwell, Chris, 308
Blanchfield, Joe (Philadelphia Jack O'Brian),
    209–210, 214–216
Blood of Abraham, 285–286
Bloods, 160, 164–165
Blue, David, 254
Blue Thumb Records, 31
Bobby Jimmy and the Critters, 78
Bogart, Humphrey, 69
Bomb Squad production team, 123, 180
Bone Thugs-N-Harmony, 287–291, 302,
    316–317

Bono, 6
Bowie, David, 277–278
Boyz N the Hood (movie), 181
"Boyz-N-the-Hood," 62–64, 66, 67, 69, 70, 97, 107, 110, 121, 123, 125, 129, 134
Bozzi, Bruce, 269
Brandt, Jerry, 256
Bratton, Creed, 242
Braun, Harland, 19, 144, 170, 297
Brigati, Eddie, 238
Bronfman, Samuel, 86
Brown, Rap, 235
Browne, Jackson, 254
Bruce, Lenny, 64
Buffalo Springfield, 114
Buffet, Jimmy, 256, 309
Burdon, Eric, 248, 258, 302
Bush, George H. W., 197–199
Butterfield, Paul, 251, 309
Byrds, the, 248, 258

Caballero Films, 112
Cagney, James, 125, 142
Calder, Clive, 308
Caldwell, Hank, 25
California Raisins, 128–129, 141–142
Canned Heat, 221–222, 248, 258
Capitol Records, 109–112, 129, 241
Carraby, Antoine. *See* DJ Yella
Cash, Johnny, 142
Cavaliere, Felix, 238
Central Intelligence Agency (CIA), 71
Cerami, Mark, 128–130, 132
Charbonnet, Pat, 182, 183
Chartwell Artists, 257, 261, 263, 275
Cherrington, Homer V., 93, 94, 301, 315
Chicago, 239, 248, 263
"Chin Check," 7
Chocolate, 190
"Chronic, The," 7
Chronic, The (album), 284, 285, 296
C.I.A., (Crew In Action), 51, 68, 107
Clapton, Eric, 64, 265
Clark, Dick, 253, 310
Clifford, Doug, 240
Coasters, 114
Cocker, Joe, 248
Cohen, Jerry, 242
Columbia Records, 31, 110, 111, 115, 241, 245, 251, 254
Commander, the, 209–212
Compton label, 171
Concepcion, Michael, 125, 160–164
Cook, Stu, 240

Coonce, Rick, 242
Cooper, Paul, 150
"Cop Killer," 203
Cornish, Gene, 238
Crane, Cheryl, 208
Creedence Clearwater Revival, 6, 33, 37, 194, 239–241, 258, 260–261
Creepin On Ah Come Up (album), 288, 316
Crips, 160–163, 165
Crosby, David, 304–305
Crosby, Stills, Nash & Young, 304–305
"Crossroad," 291, 301
Curry, Tracy "Trey." *See* D.O.C.

Dalitz, Morris Barney, 86–87
Danelli, Dino, 238
Danko, Rick, 233
Darin, Bobby, 114
Davis, Clive, 31, 93–94, 109, 115, 245, 251, 254–255, 308
Death Row Records, 25, 66, 186, 187, 284, 285, 287
Dee, Sandra, 94, 95
Def Jam, 35, 110
Delamaestro, Gigi, 270–271
Delaney Bonny and Friends, 251
Delicious Vinyl, 166
Delsener, Ron, 278–279, 281
DeMann, Freddie, 309
Demme, Ted, 184–185
Denver, John, 309
Deutsch, Milt, 208, 212–214
Devil Woman, 174–177
Diddley, Bo, 41
Diggers, 232
Digital Underground, 164
Disco Construction, 51
DJ Total K-Oss (aka Anthony Stewart), 172
DJ U-Neek, 288
DJ Yella (aka Antoine Carraby), 5, 22, 26, 55, 56, 67, 68, 69, 97–99, 103, 104, 106, 112, 125, 189. *See also* N.W.A., "Niggaz With Attitude"; Ruthless Records
D.M.C. (aka Darryl McDaniels), 56, 133–134
D.O.C. (aka Tracy "Trey" Curry), 9, 15, 21, 120, 125, 138–139, 150, 152, 158, 187–192, 205, 314
Doheny, Ned, 254
Domanick, Joe, 101
Donahue, Troy, 94
Doobie Brothers, 32
Doonesbury, 8–9
Doors, the, 6, 248, 263, 308
"Dopeman," 64, 67, 70, 71–72, 110, 125, 126

Dr. Dre (aka Andre Young), 56, 68, 69, 114,
    115, 125, 137, 138
    Dee Barnes and, 178
    discovery of talent by, 120
    DJ Yella and, 104, 106
    Eazy-E, relationship with, 11, 13–20, 22,
        66–67, 103–104, 282–285, 287
    finances of, 23, 293, 295
    gangsta funk, developed by, 107
    Ice Cube, relationship with, 107
    influences on, 104
    photographs of, 26, 50, 105
    physical appearance of, 147
    as producer, 104, 106–107, 119, 123, 148,
        149, 171, 184
    remixes of songs by, 70, 107, 114, 116,
        126
    turns against Heller and Ruthless, 6, 7, 9,
        25, 180, 186–189, 191, 192, 199,
        202–205
    women and, 55, 147
    work ethic of, 104
    See also N.W.A., "Niggaz With Attitude";
        Ruthless Records
Dr. Hook, 19
Dragnet (television show), 101
Dre. See Dr. Dre (aka Andre Young)
"Dre Day," 284
"Dream Team Is in the House, The," 40, 48
Dream Team Records, 44
Dudnik, Bob, 204
Duffy, Kevin Thomas, 94
Dunbar, Aynsley, 267
Dunhill Records, 242–243
Dylan, Bob, 64, 140, 212, 232, 234, 251, 309

E.1999 Eternal (album), 288, 290, 291,
    301–302, 316–317
Eagles, the, 256, 309
Earth, Wind & Fire, 309
Eazy-Duz-It (album), 70, 104, 107, 121, 130,
    132, 137, 140, 150, 313
Eazy-E (aka Eric Wright)
    Bush luncheon and, 197–199
    cars, houses, and office of, 165–166,
        175–177, 185, 201
    character of, 72
    death of, 79, 297–300
    Dre, relationship with, 11, 13–20, 22,
        66–67, 103–104, 282–285, 287
    drugs issue and, 71–74, 200
    estate of, 301
    family court affairs of, 177

Eazy-E (continued)
    favorite movies of, 112–113, 183–184
    female rappers and, 112–114, 146, 285
    finances of, 117–119, 138, 152, 165, 284
    first meeting with Heller, 60–65, 72–76
    generosity of, 113
    Ice Cube, relationship with, 11, 282–283,
        287, 294
    personal charisma of, 79
    photographs of, 12, 145, 159, 283
    physical appearance of, 15, 60
    police and, 98–100, 102, 169–170
    promotion by, 122
    recruitment of D.O.C., 120
    on skinhead hit list, 144
    Suge Knight and, 14–21, 24, 25
    weapons and, 165, 199–200
    women and, 137–138, 147, 173–177,
        299
    See also N.W.A., "Niggaz With Attitude";
        Ruthless Records
Eckstein, Billy, 212
Edwards, Don, 144, 146
Efil4zaggin (album), 140, 199, 202, 315–316
Egyptian Lover, 47, 78
"8 Ball," 64, 67, 70, 126
Elektra Records, 31, 76, 112, 149, 308
Ellis, Terry, 246, 248, 260
Entner, Warren, 242, 244
Ertegun, Ahmet, 114, 150, 253, 254, 308
Erving, Julius, 55
Evans, Faith, 148
Everlast, 146
Ewng, JR, 8
"Express Yourself," 126

Fab 5 Freddy, 184
FBI (Federal Bureau of Investigation),
    141–144, 146, 154, 157, 203
Fila Fresh Crew, 120
Fischel, Don, 257, 275
Fishburne, Laurence, 113, 181
Fleetwood Mac, 248
Flesh N Bone (aka Stan Howse), 287, 289–290
Fogelberg, Dan, 254–255
Fogerty, John, 6, 239–241, 260–262
Fogerty, Tom, 239
Ford, Jack, 200
"Formula, The," 150
Franklin, Aretha, 114, 115, 148
Fratianno, Jimmy "The Weasel," 208, 209
Freeway Rick, 125
Fried, David, 208

Frost, 297
"Fuck tha Police," 123–124, 126, 130, 131, 141,
    142, 144, 154–157, 198, 203

Game, the, 8
"Gangsta Gangsta," 123, 124
Ganzi, Wally, 269, 270
Gates, Daryl, 101–102
Gaye, Marvin, 37, 147, 227–229, 241
Geffen, David, 29, 58, 60, 73, 109, 115,
    251–257, 304, 308, 309
Gershon, Freddie, 19, 20, 275
"Get Together," 304–306
Giant Records, 256
Gibson, Bobby, 251–252, 261, 267, 269–271
Glaser, Joe, 216, 222, 224
Glencoe, 245
Go Mack (aka Arthur Goodman), 172
Gold, Steve, 259
Golden, Peter, 275
Gooding, Cuba, Jr., 181
Gordy, Berry, Jr., 49, 225–226, 308
Gotti, John, 167
Graham, Bill, 109, 247–250, 255, 266–267, 278, 310
Graham, Don, 31
"Grand Finale, The," 139
Grandmaster Flash, 35
Grant, Peter, 257, 309
Grass Roots, 33, 53, 242–244
Grateful Dead, 53, 248
Great Western Gramophone, 245
Greenberg, Jerry, 114–116, 148–149
Gregory, Atron, 135, 153, 154, 172
Griffey, Dick, 13, 203, 260
Grill, Rob, 242
Grodin, Jay, 170
Grogan, Emmett, 232–235
Grossman, Albert, 251–252, 309
Gruber, "Miami" Mike, 277–278, 310
Guess Who, 257, 277, 309
Gunne, Jo Jo, 254
Guns N' Roses, 122, 194

Hakim, Ned, 212–213
Harrison, George, 6, 235
Hatty O, 125
H.B.O., 69
Heller, Dave, 80–91
Heller, Hilda Kaufman, 80, 85, 88
Heller, Pete, 84–85
Heller-Fischel, 275, 276
Hell's Angels, 258, 260
Hemingway, Ernest, 42

Hendrix, Jimi, 53, 64, 230, 258, 260, 265
High Powered Productions, 104, 121, 139
Hill, Lauryn, 148
Hill, Walter, 183
Hinojosa, Jorge, 51
Hit a Lick Records, 8
Hite, Bob "the Bear," 221, 222
Hitler, Adolf, 29
Holzman, Jac, 31, 308
Hopkins, Nicky, 245
Hopp, Marty, 188, 189
Houston, Whitney, 148
Hudson, Rock, 36
Hughes, Mary, 276
Hulett, Tom, 310
Hunter, Don, 257, 309
Hutchinson, Rose, 179
Hütter, Ralf, 40
H.W.A.—Hos with Attitude, 285

"I Ain't Tha 1," 126
Ice Cube (aka O'Shea Jackson), 22, 97, 102,
    103, 125, 171–172, 178, 186
    bigotry issue and, 136, 137, 180–181, 293
    character and personality of, 107–108, 136–137
    discovery of, 120
    Eazy-E, relationship with, 11, 282–283,
        287, 294
    finances of, 292–295
    Hollywood career of, 181
    leaves N.W.A., 119, 138, 158
    lyrics by, 67–69, 107, 108, 121, 123, 126,
        136, 158, 173–174
    turns against Heller and Ruthless, 6, 7, 9,
        118, 180–183
    See also N.W.A., "Niggaz With Attitude";
        Ruthless Records)
Ice-T, 51, 68, 164, 203
"I'd Rather Fuck You," 202
Iglesias, Julio, 31, 43
Interscope, 284
Iovine, Jimmy, 284, 309
Iron Butterfly, 114, 248
Isgro, Joe, 167, 169, 170
Island, 308
"It's Like That," 56

Jackson, Doris, 136
Jackson, Hosea, 136–137
Jackson, Jesse, 164
Jackson, Michael, 52, 54, 68, 291, 309
Jackson, O'Shea. See Ice Cube
Jacobs, Bert, 279–280

INDEX

Jagger, Mick, 111, 277
Jam, Charlie, 51
Jam Master Jay (aka Jason Mizell), 56, 133–134
James, Rick, 309
Jethro Tull, 246, 248–249, 258, 260–261
Jive, 308
J.J. Fad, "Just Jammin' Fresh and Def," 43, 46, 67, 112–117, 148, 149, 164
J.J. Fad (album), 150
Joel, Billy, 32, 285
John, Elton, 37, 206, 257, 261, 264–269, 271, 281, 304, 309
Johnson, Magic, 28, 40
Johnson, Robert, 32
Jones, George, 273
Joplin, Janis, 53, 222, 230, 251, 309
Jordan, Michael, 36, 40
Julio G, 57, 131, 182, 202, 297
"Just Don't Bite It," 184

Kagan, Jeff, 177
Kaufman, Philip, 230
KDAY (radio station), 56–57, 122, 131
Kellman, Jack, 66, 220–221, 230, 232, 268
Kennedy, John F., 96, 207
Kennedy, Joseph, 86
Kenner, David, 203, 204
Kid Frost, 33
Kid N' Play, 135
King, Jay, 51
King of New York (movie), 112–113, 184
Kirschner, Don, 310
KJ, 153–154, 156, 160–162, 300
Klein, Marty, 209, 212, 213
Klein, Mike, 167, 193, 204, 283, 289, 297
Kleinman, Morris, 88
K.M.G. the Illustrator (aka Kevin Gulley), 172
Knight, Marion "Sugar Bear," 6, 9, 14–21, 24, 66, 174, 190–194, 199, 203, 260, 284, 285, 294–296
Knight Life Productions, 25
Kool DJ Herc, 35
Korshak, Sidney, 214, 216, 222–225, 258, 262
Kraftwerk, 40
Krasnow, Bob, 31, 139, 270, 309
Krayzie Bone (aka Anthony Henderson), 287
Kru-Cut Records, 44, 51
K-tel Entertainment, 128, 129
Kurz, Jules, 19
Kwamé, 135

L.A. Dre, 135, 148
L.A. Dream Team, 39, 40, 42, 46, 47, 56, 57, 77

LAPD (Los Angeles Police Department), 98–102, 165, 297
Lasker, Jay, 243–245
Layzie Bone (aka Steve Howse), 287, 288, 291
Led Zeppelin, 114, 257, 309
Lench Mob, 180, 282
Lennon, John, 6, 266, 302
"Let's Spend the Night Together," 111
Levine, Stu, 267
L'il E, 302
LiPuma, Tommy, 31
Little, Lawson, 89
Little Richard, 41
Livin' Like Hustlers (album), 171, 315
LL Cool J, 135, 157

Mack, Gregg, 57, 131
MacMillan, Don, 38–40, 42–46, 57, 58, 61, 121, 130
Macola Records, 34, 37–49, 51, 53, 57, 58, 61–62, 67, 69, 74, 83, 107, 114, 121, 130, 304
Madonna, 33, 309
Mancini, Henry, 35
Manson, Charles, 29, 230–232, 305
Manuel, Richard, 233
Mapplethorpe, Robert, 143
Marc, John, 245
Mardin, Arif, 249
Markie, Biz, 94
Marley, Bob, 308
Martin, George, 30
Marx, Groucho, 89
Maxwell, Larry "Max," 227, 245
Mayfield Road Mob, 86
Mazur, Bret, 285–286
MC Hammer, 47, 52–53, 164
MC Ren (aka Lorenzo Patterson), 5, 22, 60, 61, 120, 123, 125–127, 171, 178, 189. *See also* N.W.A., "Niggaz With Attitude"; Ruthless Records
MCA Music, 110, 149, 256, 301
McCartney, Paul, 6, 266, 302
M.C.J.B. (aka Juana Burns), 113
Melcher, Terry, 231
Mellow Man Ace, 33, 297
Metallica, 122, 194
Michaels, Lee, 238, 248, 263, 264, 276
Michel'le (album), 150, 314–315
Michel'le (aka Michelle Toussaint), 15, 21, 23, 105, 146–149, 164, 191, 192, 314–315
Miles, Buddy, 260
Miller, Mitch, 35
Minto, Janet (aka Janet Planet), 273, 276, 277
Mirage Music, 115

Mitchell, Joni, 32, 255, 256, 304, 305
Mixmasters, 56
Moffat, Tom, 239
Monster Cody, 125
Moody Blues, 309
Morris, Doug, 149, 309
Morrison, Jim, 6, 230
Morrison, Van, 19, 37, 194, 273–281, 304
Moss, Jerry, 31, 32, 77, 308
Motown, 49, 149, 225–227, 243, 245
MTV, 33, 184, 310
Musselwhite, Charlie, 33

Nash, Graham, 305
Nate Dogg, 185
Newman, Paul, 89
Newman, Randy, 60
Newton, Huey, 235–237
Nicklaus, Jack, 90
"Niggaz and Jewz (Some Say Kikes)," 285
Nixon, Richard, 305
"No More Fun and Games," 8
"No More Lies," 148–149
No One Can Do It Better (album), 139, 140,
    150, 314
"No Vaseline," 7, 9, 118, 136, 180, 181
NSYNC, 308
N.W.A., "Niggaz With Attitude"
    Arabian Prince leaves, 119
    attitude of, 100
    beginning of end of, 153, 154, 157–158
    concerts and tours by, 131–132, 134–138,
        143, 148, 153–158, 160–162
    D.O.C.'s accident, 150, 152, 158
    Eazy-Duz-It by, 70, 104, 107, 121, 130, 132,
        137, 140, 150, 313
    Efil4zaggin by, 140, 199, 202, 315–316
    end of, 25, 205
    gang factions and, 163–165
    misogyny issue, 172–174, 177
    No One Can Do It Better by, 139, 140, 150, 314
    N.W.A. and the Posse by, 70, 103, 107, 109,
        126, 139, 173, 312
    100 Miles and Runnin' by, 183, 184
    photograph of, 3
    rejections and, 109–112, 129
    Straight Outta Compton by, 5, 6, 104, 121,
        123–127, 130–133, 138, 140, 141, 150,
        173, 183, 202, 313–314
    success of, 22–24, 133–134, 138
    See also Eazy-E (aka Eric Wright); Ruthless
        Records
N.W.A. and the Posse, 67, 68

N.W.A. and the Posse (album), 70, 103, 107,
    109, 126, 139, 173, 312
Nyro, Laura, 251, 252

100 Miles and Runnin' (album), 183, 184
O'Rourke, Steve, 249, 257, 309
Ostin, Mo, 31, 32, 109, 115, 164, 203, 308
O'Sullivan, Gilbert, 94
Otis, Johnny, 53

Pardee, Rudy, 39–40, 42, 44, 45, 48, 49, 58, 71, 77
Parker, Colonel, 75
Parker, William, 101–102
Parr, Russ, 78
Pasternak, Boris, 131
Patterson, Lorenzo. See MC Ren
Percy Faith Orchestra, 95
Perenchio, Jackie Thaxton, 263, 264
Perenchio, Jerry, 257, 258, 261, 263, 264, 311
Perry, Richard, 31, 43
Peters, Jon Pagano, 215
Phillips, Bobby, 214–216, 223, 224, 261–262
Phillips, John, 243
Phillips, Johnny, 44–45, 121, 129
Phillips, Sam, 45
Pink Floyd, 37, 249, 257, 309
Platters, the, 41
Pointer Sisters, 309
Pollack, Phyllis, 122, 143
Pope, Jody, 94
Power of a Woman (album), 171
Premier Talent, 254, 257
Presley, Elvis, 45, 75, 113, 124, 309
Prince, 52, 54, 68, 309
Priority Records, 128, 129, 141, 144, 182, 183
Profile Records, 110
Public Enemy, 35, 123, 180
Puckett, Gary, 53
Purim, Flora, 66
Purple Rain (movie), 52
"Push It," 113

Racketeer Influenced and Corrupt Organizations
    Act (RICO), 72
Raft, George, 69
Rakim, 120
"Rapper's Delight," 35
Rascals, the, 33, 238–239, 241, 258, 262
"Real Niggaz Don't Die," 202
Redding, Otis, 37, 194, 248, 265, 271, 281, 302
Reebok Corporation, 164
Rhone, Sylvia, 139, 149, 309
Richards, Susan, 252, 310

Ripp, Artie, 32, 285
Roberts, Bobby, 243
Roberts, Eliot, 251, 309
Roberts, Virgil, 203
Rock, Chris, 5, 139
Roddenberry, Gene, 101
Rodney O & Joe Cooley, 47, 78
Rolling Stones, 6, 56, 111, 114, 124
Rooney, Mickey, 212–213
Rose, Howard, 257, 309
Roselli, Johnny, 208, 219
Ross, "Freeway" Rick, 36
Rubin, Rick, 35, 110
"Rumors," 51
Run (aka Joey Simmons), 56, 133–134
Run-D.M.C., 35, 55, 110, 133–134
Ruthless Records
  artists signed by, 78–79, 171–172, 287–291
  beginnings of, 60–65, 72–76
  Bone Thugs-N-Harmony and, 287–291,
    316–317
  end of, 300, 302
  FBI letter to, 141–144, 146, 154, 157, 203
  finances of, 6, 118, 138, 284, 292–295
  first major-label deal, 115–116
  Ice Cube leaves, 119
  J.J. Fad, "Just Jammin' Fresh and Def" and,
    112–117, 148
  Livin' Like Hustlers, 171, 315
  Michel'le, 150, 314–315
  money for start-up, 72, 73
  1987–88 recording sessions, 97–98, 103,
    104, 106–107, 109
  offices of, 112, 165–166
  promotion of, 121–123
  success of, 146, 150, 172
  Suge Knight and, 14–21, 24–25, 190–194
  See also Eazy-E (aka Eric Wright); N.W.A.,
    "Niggaz With Attitude"

Salt-N-Pepa, 35, 113
Sam & Dave, 204
Santana, 248
Sassy C (aka Michelle Franklin), 113
Saturday Night! (album), 68
Schaeffer, Bob, 200
Schiffman, Todd, 208
Schneider-Esleban, Florian, 40
Schoolly D, 68
Schweitzman, Alfie, 232–233
Seale, Bobby, 235
Select-O-Hits, 44, 121, 129
Selsky, Ira, 192, 204, 244
Sessions, William, 144

Sgt. Pepper's Lonely Hearts Club Band (album),
  30, 31
"She Swallowed It," 202
Shimmel, Mark, 302
"Short People," 60
Simmons, Russell, 35, 110
Sinatra, Frank, 77, 83, 111, 309
Singleton, Ernie, 301
Singleton, John, 181
Sir Jinx, 107
"Six in the Morning," 68
Slick Rain, 120
Sloan, P.F., 242
Smith, Donovan "Dirtbiker," 69, 97–98, 104
Smith, Joe, 31, 32, 58, 109–112, 115, 130, 308
Smith, Will, 146
Snake-Puppy (aka Chris Wilson), 39
Snoop Dogg, 7, 185, 302
S.O.L.A.R., Sounds of Los Angeles Records, 13,
  15, 25, 199, 260
"Something 2 Dance 2," 126
Sonny and Cher, 114
Sony Records, 15, 17, 25
Spears, Britney, 308
Spector, Phil, 31, 106, 235
"Spida Man," 7
Springsteen, Bruce, 19–20, 275
Stalin, Joseph, 36
Standells, the, 217
Star Trek, 101
Stein, Howard, 311
Steiner, Gayle, 194–197, 201, 297–298, 300, 303
Stellini, Joe, 218
Steppenwolf, 279
Stereo Cru, 68
Stern, Howard, 36
Stevens, Cat, 32
Stills, Stephen, 305
Stompanato, Johnny, 208–209, 219
Str8 off tha Streetz of Muthaphukkin Compton
  (album), 317
Straight Outta Compton (album), 5, 6, 104,
  121, 123–127, 130–133, 138, 140, 141,
  150, 173, 183, 202, 313–314
"Straight Outta Compton" (single), 123, 138
Straight Outta Compton (video), 184, 310
Stromberg, Gary, 230, 232
Sugarhill Gang, 35
Suicidal Tendencies, 122
Summer Place, A (movie), 94–95
Sun Records, 45
"Supersonic," 67, 114–117, 148, 149
Supersonic (album), 312–313
Supremes, the, 225, 227

Sweeney, Ron, 299
"Sweet Child O' Mine," 122
Sweet Thursday, 245

Tairrie B, 146, 171
Tarleton, Don, 246
Tate, Sharon, 232
Taupin, Bernie, 266
Taylor, James, 266
Taylor, Skip, 221–222
Teller, Al, 110, 146
Temptations, the, 49, 52, 103, 225, 227
Thompson, Hunter S., 8–9, 41
Thompson, Jimmy, 90
Thorpe, Jim, 84
Three Dog Night, 239, 279
Thriller (album), 52, 291
"Thuggish Ruggish Bone," 288, 290, 291
Tim Dogg, 94
Timex Social Club, 47, 51
"To Kill a Hooker," 202
Toddy Tee, 102
Toker (aka Little Beaver), 297, 300
Tone Lōc, 164, 166, 167
Tony C, 288
Tony G, 57, 131, 297
Too Short, 135
Trower, Robin, 246
Trudeau, Gary, 9
Tupac Shakur, 66, 108, 135, 164
"Turn Out the Lights," 148
Turner, Bryan, 128–132, 137, 138, 141–142, 182–183
Turner, Ike, 234–237, 248, 258
Turner, Lana, 209
Turner, Reggie (Big Reg), 9
Turner, Tina, 234, 235, 248, 258
Tyroler, Jo, 84

"U Can't Touch This," 52
U2, 6, 308
Uncle Jam's Army, 56
Uncle Sam's Curse (album), 285
Union Gap, 53
Universal Music Group, 149, 309
Unknown DJ (aka Andre Manuel), 78, 186

Vanilla Ice, 190
Viacom, 184

Wagner, Honus, 84
Waits, Tom, 150, 296
Wald, Jeff, 251
Walken, Christopher, 112–113
Wallace, Angela, 204

Warner Brothers, 31, 32, 76, 109, 114, 115, 139, 203, 241, 301, 308
Warner Music Group, 116
Warner-Seven Arts, 114
Warren G, 185
Warriors, The (movie), 183–184
Wasserman, Lew, 29
"We Had to Tear This Muthafucka Up," 181
"We Want Eazy," 121
Webb, Jack, 101
Weinberger, Billy, 88
Weiner, Danny, 255
Weintraub, Jerry, 309
Weiskopf, Tom, 89, 90
We're All in the Same Gang (album), 164
West, Mae, 143
Weston, Doug, 267–268
Wexler, Jerry, 115
Wexler, Mushy, 88
White Heat (movie), 125, 142
Whitman, Charles, 230
Who, the, 248
"Wild Thing," 166
Wilde, Oscar, 11
Wiley, Charles, 147, 178
Will 1X (aka William Adams), 286
William Morris Agency, 19, 29, 251, 262
Williams, Alonzo, 26, 48–49, 51–56, 58–61, 66–69, 71, 78, 103–104, 107
Williams, Tasha, 288
Williams, Tookie, 125, 160
Wilson, Allan, 221, 222
Wilson, Jackie, 41
Winter, Johnny, 258
Wish Bone (aka Charles Scruggs), 287
Wolf and Epic, 285–286
World Class Wreckin' Crew, 26, 51–56, 58, 66, 68, 78, 97, 103, 107, 148
"World Without Love," 266
Wright, Chris, 260
Wright, Eric. See Eazy-E

Yano, Steve, 47–48, 56
Yo! MTV Raps, 184
Young, Andre. See Dr. Dre
Young, Doug, 61, 121–122
Young, Jesse Colin, 304, 305
Young, Mona Lisa, 26
Young, Neil, 32, 255, 256, 305
Youngbloods, 304, 305

Zaentz, Saul, 240
Zappa, Frank, 32